# LEADING MARINES

# LEADING MARINES

## U.S. MARINE CORPS

MCWP 6-11

A MARINE CORPS BOOK

For administrative purposes,
FMFM 1-0 is reidentified as MCWP 6-11.

**A MARINE CORPS BOOK**

Published by Wildside Press LLC.
www.wildsidebooks.com

DEPARTMENT OF THE NAVY
Headquarters United States Marine Corps
Washington, D.C. 20380-1775

3 January 1995

# FOREWORD

The most important responsibility in our Corps is leading Marines. If we expect Marines to lead and if we expect Marines to follow, we must provide the education of the heart and of the mind to win on the battlefield and in the barracks, in war and in peace. Traditionally, that education has taken many forms, often handed down from Marine to Marine, by word of mouth and by example.

Our actions as Marines every day must embody the legacy of those who went before us. Their memorial to us—their teaching, compassion, courage, sacrifices, optimism, humor, humility, commitment, perseverance, love, guts, and glory—is the pattern for our daily lives. This manual attempts to capture those heritages of the Marine Corps' approach to leading. It is not prescriptive because there is no formula for leadership. It is not all-inclusive because to capture all that it is to be a Marine or to lead Marines defies pen and paper. Instead, it is intended to provide those charged with leading Marines a sense of the legacy they have inherited, and to help them come to terms with their own personal leadership style. The indispensable condition of Marine Corps leadership is action and attitude, not words. As one Marine leader said, "Don't tell me how good you are. Show me!"

Marines have been leading for over 200 years and today continue leading around the globe. Whether in the field or in garrison, at the front or in the rear, Marines, adapting the time-honored values, traditions, customs, and history of our Corps to their generation, will continue to lead—and continue to win.

This manual comes to life through the voices, writings, and examples of not one person, but many. Thousands of Americans who have borne, and still bear, the title "Marine" are testimony that "Once a Marine, Always a Marine" and "Semper Fidelis" are phrases that define our essence. It is to those who know, and to those who will come to know, this extraordinary way of life that this book is dedicated.

C. E. MUNDY, Jr.
General, U.S. Marine Corps
Commandant of the Marine Corps

DISTRIBUTION: 139 000001 00

# Leading Marines

## Appendices

*Marine Corps Manual*, Paragraph 1100 — Core Values — Leadership Traits — Leadership Principles — The Oaths — Trust

## Notes

# Introduction

*Leading Marines* describes a leadership philosophy that reflects our traditional strengths as an institution and attempts to define the very ethos of being a Marine. It is about the inseparable relationship between the leader *and* the led, and is as much about the individual Marine—the bedrock upon which our Corps is built—as it is about any leader. There is less a line between the leader and the led than *a bond.* It is also about the Corps; about that unspoken feeling among Marines that is more than tradition or the cut of the uniform. It flows from the common but unique forge from which Marines come, and it is about the undefinable spirit that forms the character of our Corps. It draws from the shared experiences of danger, violence, the adrenaline of combat, and the proximity to death. All of this is based upon certain fundamental traits and principles of leading. Marines are not born knowing them, but must learn what they are and what they represent.

When teaching Marines, we have always drawn from a wealth of material that lies in our heritage and in our traditions. To capture some of that legacy, this manual begins with a chapter on *our ethos*, a chapter that attempts to iden- tify just what it is that makes Marines. Being a Marine, after all, is different, and, therefore, leading Marines is differ- ent from leading in any other walk of life. It must be different because of who and what we are and what we do. It is different because of the character of our Corps—a char- acter that lies at the very foundation of individual cama- raderie, unit cohesion, and combat effectiveness. It is this character—our ethos—that gives Marines the pride, con- fidence, and hardness necessary to win.

Winning means victory in daily life as well as in combat. If a Marine fails to uphold our standards and dishonors oneself or our Corps in peacetime by failing to support fellow Marines, by failing to do his or her best to accomplish the task at hand, or by failing to follow ethical standards in daily life, how can we expect that same Marine to uphold these critical foundations of our Corps in the searing cauldron of combat?

Thus, the most fundamental element of leading Marines is to understand what it is to be a Marine, and it is on this understanding that we begin.

The second chapter focuses on the *foundations* of Marine Corps leadership—our core values, and the leadership traits and principles that are taught to every Marine. These are the ethical standards by which all Marines are judged. They are, ultimately, why Marines fight.

The third chapter helps Marines understand some of the *challenges* to leading and discusses how Marines can overcome them. It relies on the stories of Marine heroes—some well known, others not so well known—to serve as anchors that show Marine character and vividly depict, through action, what is required to lead Marines.

Our leadership style is a unique blend of service ethos and time-tested concepts that support Marine leaders in peace and war. The *epilogue* summarizes our discussion of leading Marines and asks Marines to spend time in reflection, looking closely at their legacy, at who and what we are, and at who and what they are.

Inescapably, this manual is based on the firm belief that, as others have said in countless ways, our Corps embodies the spirit and essence of those who have gone before. It is about the belief, shared by all Marines, that there is no higher calling than that of a United States Marine. It is about the traditions of our Corps that we rely upon to help us stay the course and continue the march when the going gets tough. It is about a "band of brothers"—men and women of every race and creed—who epitomize in their daily actions the core values of our Corps: *honor*, *courage*, *commitment*.

It is about Marines.

## Chapter 1

# Our Ethos

*"Marine human material was not one whit better than that of the human society from which it came. But it had been hammered into form in a different forge, hardened with a different fire. The Marines were the closest thing to legions the nation had. They would follow their colors from the shores of home to the seacoast of Bohemia, and fight well at either place."*

*"A Marine Corps officer was still an officer, and a sergeant behaved the way good sergeants had behaved since the time of Caesar, expecting no nonsense, allowing none. And Marine leaders had never lost sight of their primary—their only—mission, which was to fight."*

— T. R. Fehrenbach

Being a Marine is a state of mind. It is an experience some have likened more to a calling than a profession. Being a Marine is not a job—not a pay check; it is not an occupational specialty. It is not male or female, majority or minority; nor is it a rank insignia. Stars, bars, or chevrons are only indicators of the responsibility or authority we hold at a given time. Rather, being a Marine comes from the eagle, globe, and anchor that is tattooed on the soul of every one of us who wears the Marine Corps uniform. It is a searing mark in our innermost being which comes after the rite of passage through boot camp or Officer Candidates School when a young man or woman is allowed for the first time to say, "I'm a United States Marine." And unlike physical or psychological scars, which, over time, tend to heal and fade in intensity, the eagle, globe, and anchor only grow more defined—more intense—the longer you are a Marine. "Once a Marine, always a Marine."

"Among Marines there is a fierce loyalty to the Corps that persists long after the uniform is in mothballs. . . . Woven through that sense of belonging, like a steel thread, is an elitist spirit. Marines are convinced that, being few in number, they are selective, better, and, above all, different.[2]"

This matter of being different lies at the heart of our leadership philosophy and has been nourished over the years by combining the characteristics of soldiers, sailors, and airmen. The result is a sea soldier—an odd conglomeration that talks like one, dresses like another, and fights like them all. The determination to be different, and remain different, has manifested itself in many ways over the years—from military appearance, to strict obedience to orders, to disciplined behavior, to adherence to traditional standards, and most of all, to an unyielding conviction that we exist to fight. Marines have been distinguished by these characteristics from the beginning. A sense of elitism has grown "from the fact that every Marine, whether enlisted or officer, goes through the same training experience. Both the training of recruits and the basic education of officers—going back to 1805—have endowed the Corps with a sense of cohesiveness enjoyed by no other American service."[3]

This matter of being different is at the very heart of leading Marines. It defines who and what we are by reflecting the mystical cords of the mind that bind all Marines. What we are, what we have been, what Marines will always be, is enduring.

There is yet another element of being different that defines Marines, and that is selflessness: a spirit that places the self-interest of the individual second to that of the institution we know as the Corps. That selflessness is stronger nowhere in American society than among Marines.

Our ethos has been shaped by ordinary men and women—heroes who showed extraordinary leadership and courage, both physical and moral, as they shaped the special character that is the essence of our Corps. They are heroes and leaders who are remembered not by their names, or rank, or because they received a decoration for valor. They are remembered because they were Marines.

The story is told that in June 1918, during the First World War, an American lady visited one of the field hospitals behind the French Army. "It happened that occasional casualties of the Marine Brigade . . . were picked up by French stretcher-bearers and evacuated to French hospitals. And this lady, looking down a long, crowded ward, saw on a pillow a face unlike the fiercely whiskered Gallic heads there displayed in rows. She went to it. 'Oh,' she said, 'surely, you are an American!' 'No, ma'am,' the casualty answered, 'I'm a Marine.[4] "

Sixty-five years later, a veteran of the terrorist bombing in Beirut stood amidst the rubble, carnage, and despair surrounding his fallen comrades, barraged by questions from news reporters. "Should you be here? Should anyone be here? Should the United States pull out?" The young lance corporal's answer was straightforward: "Where else should I be? I'm a United States Marine. If anyone must be here, it should be Marines."

Another Beirut veteran, wounded and evacuated to a hospital in Germany, unable to talk or see, was visited by the Commandant. As the general stooped beside the Marine to say a few words of comfort into his ear, the lance corporal reached up to feel the stars to make sure that the man talking to him was who he claimed to be. Unable to see or speak, weak from a concussion and other injuries, the young Marine motioned for something with which to write. He could have written anything; he could have asked for anything. Instead, he wrote, "Semper Fi"—Always Faithful. He was concerned more about his Corps and his fellow Marines than himseff.

## THE U. S. MARINE

*"Success in battle is not a function of how many show up, but who they are."*[6]

Individual Marines—like those described above—are the bedrock upon which our Corps' spirit is built. From the first day of recruit training, to their first assignments, to their first celebration of the Marine Corps birthday, each Marine is infused with an understanding of the deeds of his or her predecessors. "Recruit training, both officer and enlisted, has long been 'the genesis of the enduring sense of brotherhood that characterizes the Corps.' New recruits are told the day they enter training that, as one Marine leader put it, 'A Marine believes in his God, in his Country, in his Corps, in his buddies, and in himself.' "[7] What happens on the parade decks of Parris Island and San Diego or in the woods of Quantico is what *makes* Marines—it is the instillation of "an intangible *esprit* along with the complicated, specific knowledge of soldiering."[8]

Marines undergo a personal transformation at recruit training. There, they receive more than just superb training; they are ingrained with a sense of service, honor, and discipline. It is there, as a former recruit depot Commanding General said, that Marines develop a "sense of brotherhood, interdependence, and determination to triumph." The Corps' history is full of tales of individual triumphs—Daly, Butler, Puller, Basilone, Streeter, Huff, Vargas, Petersen, Wilson, Barrow, and countless others—that exhibit the indomitable spirit of Marines in combat and in surmounting day-to-day challenges. Sustaining that spirit are "old battles, long forgotten, that secured our nation . . . scores of skirmishes, far off, such as Marines have nearly every year . . . traditions of things endured and things accomplished, such as regiments hand down forever.[9]"

This spirit was clearly evident in the dark, opening days of the Korean War. In July 1950, the 1st Provisional Marine Brigade was rushed to Korea to assist the Army in stemming the North Korean tide. In August, a British military observer of the desperate fighting in and around Miryang sent the following dispatch: "The situation is critical and Miryang may be lost. The enemy has driven a division-sized salient across the Naktong. More will cross the river tonight. If Miryang is lost . . . we will be faced with a withdrawal from Korea. I am heartened that the Marine Brigade will move against the Naktong Salient tomorrow. They are faced with impossible odds, and I have no valid reason to substantiate it, but I have the feeling they will halt the enemy. . . . These Marines have [a] swagger, confidence, and hardness. . . . Upon this thin line of reasoning, I cling to the hope of victory.[10]"

The following morning, the Marines attacked under the close air support of Marine gull-winged Corsairs. Two of the lead battalion's undermanned "thin rifle companies pushed across the open rice fields" and "up the steep ridge. Three times the Marines reached the top; three times they" were thrown back. The fourth time, they stayed[11].

The Marines faced a night of repeated infiltrations and a series of hard attacks. As dawn approached, it became evident that the Marines were there to stay, and by daylight, the Communist retreat became a rout. "When night descended again . . . the only North Koreans left in the Naktong Bulge were dead ones amid the flotsam of a wrecked division. Thirty-four large-caliber artillery pieces were taken by the brigade. . . . Enemy casualties exceeded 4,000." [12] The "thin line" carried the day not because they had the strength of numbers or firepower; they carried the day because they were Marines.

The spirit of the past continues today as new heroes step forward to take their place in the pantheon. It lives on in such phrases as "semper fidelis," "uncommon valor," "every Marine a rifleman," and "first to fight." Esprit, aggressiveness, and courage are the essence of our Corps.

Marines, as they always have, carry on that tradition as a force in readiness, able and willing to go anywhere and do anything. "Trained men who will stand and fight are never obsolete. It was not the bowman, but the long bow, not the cavalryman, but the horse, which vanished from the scene.

Men—the man, the individual who is the Marine Corps symbol and stock-in-trade—constitute the one element which never changes."[13]

## Every Marine a Rifleman

There is both a practical and moral dimension to the credo "every Marine a rifleman."[14] The force structure of the Corps reflects its central purpose: an expeditionary force in readiness. And because it is expeditionary, it is also austere. Austerity places a premium on the role of every Marine. There are no "rear area" Marines, and no one is very far from the fighting during expeditionary operations. The success of each of these operations depends on the speed and flexibility with which Marines build combat power. Marines fighting with maneuver elements are backed up by fellow Marines who labor unceasingly to support the mission by building logistic bases, running truck convoys, distributing supplies, and fighting when needed to.

This is nothing new. The first Marine aviator to earn the Medal of Honor in World War II, Captain Henry "Hank" Elrod, was a fighter pilot on Wake Island. His aircraft destroyed after 15 days of heroic defense of the island, he died leading a platoon of Marines. Actions of Marines like Captain Elrod, and others, continue to demonstrate that every

Marine is a rifleman. These actions occur with such regularity, that non-Marines often show surprise on learning that there are any specialties in the Corps other than the infantry. This perception on the part of others is part of what makes the Corps the Corps and transcends the issue of occupational specialties.

There is almost nothing more precious to a Marine than a fellow Marine. This traditional bond flows from the combat training which all Marines receive, officer and enlisted, and the shared danger and adversity inherent in expeditionary operations.

***"Those men on the line were my family, my home. They were closer to me than I can say, closer than any friends had been or ever would be. They had never let me down, and I couldn't do it to them. I had to be with them, rather than let them die and me live with the knowledge that I might have saved them. Men, I now knew, do not fight for flag or country, for the Marine Corps or glory or any other abstraction. They fight for one another. Any man in combat who lacks comrades who will die for him, or for whom he is willing to die, is not a man at all. He is truly damned."*** [15]

This cohesion between Marines is not a function of a particular unit within the Corps. It is a function of the Corps *itself.* When a Marine reports to a unit, he or she may be unknown personally, but is a known quantity professionally.

Regardless of anything else known about them, their leaders know that they have been trained as Marines and that they bear, consequently, that indelible stamp of "rifleman."

Nowhere is the effect of this more evident than when Marines are exposed to danger or to war. Fellow Marines, remote from the action, are usually uneasy. Marines are going in harm's way, and there is an unnatural feeling of being "left out" among those not able to go. This attitude is born of the confidence that every Marine can fight, that every Marine can contribute to the mission, and that every Marine is duty bound to share in the danger and the risk of every other Marine in the Corps. One Marine father sending his son into the Corps summed it up this way: "May our Corps not have to go in harm's way on your watch; but if it does, may you never be the second Marine there."

This "spirit of confidence comes from training and tradition; . . . each individual Marine, because of the fighting tradition of the Corps and the toughness of the training, is confident of his own ability and that of his buddies. That is why Marines fight with discipline and steadfastness in the toughest situations, when victory or survival becomes doubtful, why they turn to their belief in themselves, their buddies, and their units, fighting for one another, their unit, and the Marine Corps. This confidence in themselves and one another very often spells the difference between victory and survival and defeat and annihilation. Service with the Marine Corps means service with a team. Everything that the Marine Corps does is a team effort.

Every unit from the Marine expeditionary force down to the fire team is organized into a team—a group of highly select, well-trained Marines all pointed to one objective. During the fight out from the frozen Chosin in 1950, a military observer watched with astonishment as gunners from a Marine Artillery gun crew integrated with cooks, bakers, and clerks to form a rifle platoon under the command of a lieutenant from motor transport, functioned perfectly as part of a rifle company. Many times . . . the success of the entire movement depended on the fighting ability of a single platoon or company. In many cases these units were made up of Marines and subordinate units that the day before were in another command. The success of the whole operation was possible only through the local successes of the small units. The small units were successful because individual Marines are team players, trained to handle themselves in any situation and to subordinate their own desires to the objectives of the team.[16]

The sense that every Marine is a rifleman, demonstrated at the Chosin Reservoir and in a hundred other places, is at the heart of the ethos of the Corps. This unspoken feeling among Marines is more than tradition, or the cut of the uniform. It is the reality and adrenaline of a shared experience of danger and violence, the proximity to death, that which Oliver Wendell Holmes, a famous American Supreme Court Justice and Civil War veteran, called the "touch of fire."

To visit the Marine monument deep in Belleau Wood is to come to grips with the timeless importance of this unspoken feeling for the Marine Corps. As the shadows lengthen in that quiet glade, the image of the Marine on the monument seems to come to life, to move resolutely forward into the face of withering German fire, forever frozen in that bright June morning of 1918. In one sense, he embodies the spirit of the thousands of Marines, past and present, who have given their all for Country and Corps. But he also stands for the thousands of Marines yet to come, on whom this nation will depend for its security and to carry its flag in every clime and place. And in him, and them, there is the certainty that their sense of duty and honor will be strengthened by the assurance that every Marine is, first and foremost, a rifleman.

## SOLDIERS OF THE SEA

"Unique among soldiers of the world, Marines are accustomed to service both ashore and afloat. The Marine Corps' 'maritime character' has shaped the Corps since its inception. In 1775, Congress resolved that two battalions of Marines be raised '. . . such as are good seamen, or so acquainted with maritime affairs as to be able to serve to advantage at sea, when required.' "[17] The Congress went on to commission the first naval officer in our nation's history—the senior Marine officer of the Revolution.

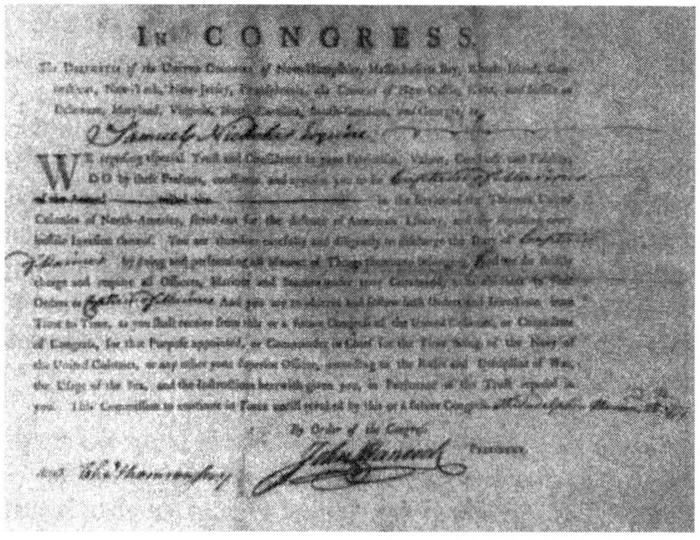

IN CONGRESS.

The historic partnership between the Navy and the Marine Corps is a heritage that continues today. The anchor in our emblem symbolizes that the individual Marine remains a maritime soldier—a "soldier of the sea." Marine officers are "naval" officers. Our aviators are "naval" aviators. As early as 1798, the Secretary of the Navy noted that the Corps' missions were of an "amphibious nature" and we have been members of the Department of the Navy since 1834. The partnership was a close one initially and grew closer over time—so close that sometimes one forgets that the Navy and Marine Corps are separate Services under the authority of a single Secretary.

Though early Marines served primarily on board ships as part of the ship's company, they always had a secondary role to serve as expeditionary forces, whenever or wherever needed. Marine Captain Samuel Nicholas' amphibious expedition to New Providence Island in the Bahamas in 1776 and Marine Lieutenant Presley O'Bannon's 1804 landing in Tripoli were the first deployments of American forces from home soil. They were the precursors to the role Marines played in World War II, Korea, Lebanon in 1958, in the Dominican Republic in 1965, in Vietnam, Lebanon again in 1982, Grenada, in Southwest Asia, and scores of other places since.

The nation was a maritime one in 1775 when Marines first crossed the quarterdecks of the Continental fleet, and it is no less today. Three quarters of the world's population lives near a coastline, and four out of five world capitals are within 300 miles of the sea. The vital relationship between the United States Navy and Marine Corps brings unique and powerful naval capabilities that are key to meeting our nation's security interests.

Ours is a world ideally suited for the employment of warriors who come from the sea, whose past and potential future battlegrounds are mainly in the "watery maze," green water, and coastal regions that comprise the littorals of the world. Operations along these littorals require special "training and preparation . . . along Marine Corps lines. It is not enough that the troops be skilled infantry men and jungle men or artillery men . . . they must be skilled water men and jungle men who know it can be done—Marines with Marine training.[18]"

## THE MARINE TRADITION

*"Such as regiments hand down forever."*

The individual Marine, recruit and officer candidate training, "every Marine a rifleman," and our maritime character contribute to our heritage. Separately and collectively, they set us apart from other fighting forces and are the cement that glues the Marine Corps together and gives Marines a common outlook that transcends their grade, unit, or billet. Self-image is at the heart of the Marine Corps—a complex set of ideals, beliefs, and standards that define our Corps. Our selfless dedication to and elevation of the institution over self is uncommon elsewhere.

Ultimately undefinable, this self-image sets Marines apart from others and requires a special approach to leading. Consequently, Marine leaders must be forged in the same crucible and steeled with the same standards and traditions as those placed in their charge—standards and traditions as old as our nation itself.

Those who know Marines give many reasons why America needs a Marine Corps, but first and foremost, Marines exist to fight and win.[19] From this duty, from this reason for being, everything else flows. If it doesn't, it is meaningless. This spirit is the character of our Corps. It is the foundation of our cohesion and combat effectiveness, and it gives Marines that "swagger, confidence, and hardness" necessary for victory—qualities seen in the hills of Korea and in hundreds of other engagements before and since.

Marines believe that to be a Marine is special; that those good enough to become Marines are special; and that the institution in which they are bonded is special. That is why the legion analogy is so appropriate for the Corps. Marines, far flung, performing dangerous—sometimes apparently meaningless and often overlooked missions—find strength and sense of purpose simply knowing that they are Marines in that mystical grouping they know as the Corps.

Among the five Armed Services of our nation, four have Service songs; only the Marine Corps has its Hymn. For scores of years before it became recently fashionable to stand for all Service songs, Marines always stood when our Hymn was played. And to this day, while others stand with cheers and applause to their Service song, Marines stand quietly, unwaveringly at attention, as the Hymn of their Corps is played. Marines are different.

"The 1st Marine Division, fighting its way back from the Chosin Reservoir in December 1950, was embattled amid the snows from the moment the column struck its camp at Hagaru. By midnight, after heavy loss through the day, it had bivouacked at Kotori, still surrounded, still far from the sea." The commanding general was alone in his tent. It was his worst moment. "The task ahead seemed hopeless. Suddenly he heard music." Outside, some Marines, on their way to a warming tent, were softly singing the Marines' Hymn. " 'All doubt left me,' " said the general. " 'I knew then we had it made.[20] "

For more than 200 years, the steady performance of the Marine Corps has elevated it to the epitome of military excellence. It is an elite fighting force renowned for its success in combat, esprit de corps, and readiness always to be "first to fight." "More than anything else, Marines have fought and . . . won because of a commitment—to a leader and to a small brotherhood where the ties that bind are mutual respect and confidence, shared privation, shared hazard, shared triumph, a willingness to obey, and determination to follow.[21]"

***"The man who will go where his colors go, without asking, who will fight a phantom foe in jungle and mountain range, without counting, and who will suffer and die in the midst of incredible hardship, without complaint, is still what he has always been, from Imperial Rome to sceptered Britain to democratic America. He is the stuff of which legions are made.***

***"His pride is in his colors and his regiment, his training hard and thorough and coldly realistic, to fit him for what he must face, and his obedience is to his orders. As a legionary, he held the gates of civilization for the classical world; . . . he has been called United States Marine."*** [22]

The Marine Corps' vision of leading is less concerned with rank, self-identity, recognition, or privilege than the essence of our Corps: the individual Marine and the unyielding determination to persevere because Marines and the Corps do not fail. Our vision of leading is linked directly to our common vision of warfighting, which needs leaders devoted to leading, capable of independent and bold action, who are willing and eager to assume new and sometimes daunting responsibilities, willing to take risks—not because they may succeed, but because the *Corps* must succeed.

This always has been, and always will be, what leading Marines is all about.

# Chapter 2

# Foundations

*"A spirit of comradeship and brotherhood in arms came into being in the training camps and on the battlefields. This spirit is too fine a thing to be allowed to die. It must be fostered and kept alive and made the moving force in all Marine Corps organizations."*[1]

—Major General John A. Lejeune

*"Leaders must have a strong sense of the great responsibility of their office; the resources they will expend in war are human lives."*[2]

—FMFM 1

Imagine you are a rifleman in a company ready to assault a line of enemy machine gun bunkers. You are lying flat on the ground protected for the moment by a slight rise between you and the enemy. But just above your head, the enemy's guns "are throwing a visible and audible curtain of lead, which thuds into the trees around you, causing you to wonder if it makes the same sound when it hits flesh. You tell yourself it is impossible . . . to penetrate that curtain of fire alive." Yet, in a moment, a sergeant's voice will boom, "Let's go! You can't live forever!" "But all you hear now is the clatter of the machine guns. The vision of the dead and wounded you saw on the way up to the front rises to plague you; your belly deflates and lies flat against your backbone, and all the gallant thoughts you had hoped to have at this moment are gone. You are naked and alone with the instinct of self-preservation[3]."

Why do individuals rush forward against their most basic instincts? Why do Marines take their lives in their hands and lead a charge straight into enemy guns? In World War II, what was it that made Marines clamber out of their landing craft into water of unknown depth, and charge into a hail of machine-gun and artillery fire, not knowing whether they would ever make it to the beach? In Vietnam, what was it that made a Marine "take the point" and start down the dark and misty jungle trail? In Desert Storm, what was it that made helicopter pilots fly in the smoke and oil clouds when they could not see the ground below or the sky above?

At the heart of why Marines are able to put mission accomplishment over concern for their own safety is leadership—leadership that is the combination of the intangible elements of our ethos and the more tangible elements of our leadership philosophy. These tangible elements include the *Marine Corps Manual* and our core values, leadership traits and principles, the oath all Marines take when assuming office or enlisting, and special trust and confidence. These elements are reproduced in the appendices, and it is important that Marines understand not only the concepts behind each of them, but also how they fit together so they can be used effectively by Marine leaders.

FMFM 1 describes our profession as one where leaders "are expected to be students of the art and science of war at all levels . . . with a solid foundation in military theory and a knowledge of military history and the timeless lessons to be gained from it."[4] Part of that foundation lies not only in our ethos, but is also based on the elements that help form our leadership philosophy.

These elements contain the concepts that help give direction and guidance to Marine leaders. Like blocks in an arch, each depends on others to provide support. With our core values serving as the keystone, they all serve to buttress the structure which Marines leaders may draw upon. Just as builders must use every block in the arch to support it, so too must Marine leaders use every element of our leadership foundation at their disposal. But, just as every arch is different, requiring different sizes and shapes of building blocks, every leadership challenge is different, requiring a different use and blend of the leadership foundations.

To meet these challenges, leaders must have the respect of their followers. If followers do not believe their leader is operating from a foundation of values, then words become hollow and lack credibility and the leader will be ineffective. Whether a squad leader, first sergeant, battalion commander, or force commander, a leader must embrace both the intangible and the tangible elements of our philosophy. They are the guiding beliefs and principles that give us strength, influence our attitudes, and guide our behavior. They bond the family of Marines into a force able to overcome every challenge.

All Marines pass through the crucible of our entry level training. In that harsh and uncompromising forge, their steel is tempered to withstand the stresses of future challenges even more severe and testing. It is here that we begin to lay the foundation. At the very center of this process is understanding and applying all the elements of our leadership philosophy—including our ethos. Marine leadership, wherever it is exercised, is firmly grounded in these values and must meet the demands of our unique service.

## THE UNIQUE OBLIGATIONS OF MARINE CORPS SERVICE

*"Military service is a difficult profession and it makes unique demands on each individual. Unless the Corps' leaders recognize and dedicate themselves to meeting those demands in a professional manner, the Corps will not stand ready to assist with the important role of the military—keeping the nation secure."* [5]

Our obligations as Marines to society are different. Marines adhere to a moral philosophy based on these special obligations that is also separate and more demanding than those of the larger society we serve. Our military life—the profession of arms—has been described as "the ordered application of force under an unlimited liability." [6] That means Marines must subordinate their own self-interest to the overall interest of the group. This special military obligation sets Marines apart from society as a whole. And it is this unique obligation of Marine Corps service that places special demands on Marine leaders.

From the earliest landings of the Corps, Marines have fought from the sea, with the water to their backs, and nowhere to go but forward. At places such as Guadalcanal, Tarawa, and Inchon the fighting, often desperate, usually bloody, demanded that every Marine fight and every Marine lead; there could be no other way. The bond which grows among warriors who, together, experience great danger in the crucible of war is difficult to describe. It is the steel cable that binds every Marine, one to another, and all Marines to the Corps. That every Marine is a warrior and a leader is more than a capability: *it is an attitude and a standard of excellence.*

## ESTABLISHING AND MAINTAINING STANDARDS

Maintaining this attitude and standard of excellence is a responsibility not limited to officers, staff noncommissioned officers, or noncommissioned officers. It is the responsibility of all Marines. In fact, one of the basic tenets of Marine Corps leadership is that whenever two Marines are together, of whatever grade, one is in charge.

Paragraph 1100 of the *Marine Corps Manual*, contained in the appendices, requires leaders to maintain leadership standards and identifies qualities that every leader should possess. It emphasizes that these qualities can be developed within the individual Marine, and that Marine leaders have the responsibility for developing those qualities. Concepts such as comradeship and brotherhood, teacher and scholar, and love of

Corps and country are reproduced just as Major General Commandant John Lejeune first articulated them nearly 75 years ago.

These standards, and the others contained in the appendices, are learned by all Marines in entry-level training. They provide points of departure and a yardstick from which Marines can determine their own leadership abilities and assist their subordinates. They are generally self-explanatory, and are always best discussed through the use of action-centered examples. Because they are simple concepts, they can be used to build a "short list" of actions and techniques that will assist leaders everywhere. They are straightforward and very basic, and that is their value. Although they do not guarantee success, just as the principles of war are used to help us think about warfighting, these tangible elements help us think about leadership.

These standards and ideals—from ethos to traits and principles to our core values—are recognized as essentials of good leadership. But they are only so many words unless Marine leaders breathe life into them. They do that through personal example.

## SETTING THE EXAMPLE

*"Leadership is a heritage which has passed from Marine to Marine since the founding of the Corps. . . . mainly acquired by observation, experience, and emulation. Working with other Marines is the Marine leader's school.*[7]*"*

The tradition of leadership education in our Corps since its earliest days has often been described as "leading by example." In fact, leadership, in the long run, depends upon the example set by the leader, not only as a warfighter, but also as a citizen and human being. Being in the Corps does not change this simple rule. On the contrary, because we are Marines, the effect of our example is emphasized and magnified a hundredfold. *Leaders setting the example* is far more important in the Marine Corps than in any other activity—military or civilian.[8]

A few years ago, the Commandant received a letter from a friend of the Corps. It describes as well as anyone could the importance Marine leaders put on setting the example:

"Recently I was in an air terminal. Most military people there presented a pretty sloppy appearance—coats unbuttoned, ties loosened, etc. There was a Marine corporal in uniform who was just the opposite. I spoke to the Marine and pointed out the difference to him. I asked him why it was so? His answer was: 'The Marines don't do that.'[9]"

Setting a personal example requires "high moral standards reflecting virtue, honor, patriotism, and subordination in personal behavior and in performance."[10] These are inner qualities that mark leaders. Rather than outward marks of greatness, they are often deeply buried, and, in many cases, one must look closely to see an individual's inner strengths.

For example, consider how the 13th Commandant, Major General John A. Lejeune, described Medal of Honor recipient Sergeant Major John H. Quick:

"Perhaps of all the Marines I ever knew, Quick approached more nearly the perfect type of noncommissioned officer. A calm, forceful, intelligent, loyal and courageous man he was. I never knew him to raise his voice, lose his temper, or use profane language, and yet he exacted and obtained prompt and explicit obedience from all persons subject to his or- ders.[11]"

In another example, Major General Alexander Vandegrift was awarded the Medal of Honor in 1942 for his "tenacity, courage, and resourcefulness" against a strong and determined enemy in the battle for Guadalcanal. In later years, "a character sketch of him . . . included this: 'He is so polite and so soft-spoken that he is continually disappointing the people whom he meets. They find him lacking in the fire-eating traits they like to expect of all Marines, and they find it difficult to believe that such a mild-mannered man could really have led and won the bloody fight.' When another officer spoke warmly of

Vandegrift's coolness under fire, his 'grace under pressure,' . . . he replied: 'I shouldn't be given any credit, I'm built that way.' "[12]

It is not enough that Marine leaders themselves set the example. Their followers must be equally aware of the importance of following established standards. Followership is just as important as leadership. Followers are the backbone of any effective organization because without loyal, dedicated followers there can be no effective leaders. As one leader put it, "Every Marine, from the Commandant down, is a follower. The good followers, those who may be depended on to carry out their instructions precisely, without regard to difficulty, hazard or personal risk, are the substance of the Corps. And where combat circumstance, as it often does, suddenly thrusts upon the follower the responsibilities of a leader, those who are properly indoctrinated seize the opportunity and suc- ceed.[13]"

Corporal James Barrett's actions demonstrate clearly how the followers' and the leader's responsibilities merge.

While he served as a squad leader with Company I, 3d Battalion, 26th Marines, in the Republic of Vietnam, his "company came under heavy mortar, rocket, and artillery fire followed by a supported infantry assault by a numerically superior North Vietnamese Army force. In the initial attack, numerous casualties were taken and the company was forced to withdraw to a more advantageous position. Undaunted, Corporal Barrett courageously maintained his squad's position and directed accurate counter fire against the hordes of assaulting enemy. Assuming control of the platoon when his platoon commander became a casualty, he rallied his men, reorganized the platoon and led them in an effective counterattack against the enemy. With complete disregard for his own safety, he moved from position to position, encouraging his men and resupplying them with ammunition. Unhesitatingly, he aided the wounded and directed their evacuation. During the six hour ordeal, he repositioned his men five times to thwart the enemy advance and inflicted numerous casualties on the enemy force."[14]

In the Marine Corps, we are trained to endure combat, violence, and death—along with other less arduous situations, in both peace and war. Like Corporal Barrett, we are trained to make life or death decisions over both our Marines and our enemies. In the end, the decisions we make must pass the test of ethical behavior.

Ethical behavior is action taken specifically in observance of a defined standard of conduct. For Marines, ethics are the standards of our Corps. They set forth general guidelines about what we ought to do. As a result, the individual is obligated to apply judgment to a given set of circumstances. Judgment, and therefore choice, is at the center of ethical conduct. Every Marine, regardless of grade, has this responsibility.

Ethical choices often involve a moral dilemma: the necessity to choose between competing obligations in circumstances that prevent one from doing both. But, there is more to it than this. *Action* is at the heart of ethical behavior. An academic understanding of what is right and wrong is irrelevant unless it is coupled to appropriate action. And even then, the answer is not always clear. Consider the options facing this helicopter pilot:

The pilot in command of a single aircraft was diverted for an emergency extraction of a reconnaissance team. He contacted the team and planned the approach for pick-up. Just as he landed, the aircraft began to take automatic weapons fire.

The reconnaissance team made for the helo as the fire became more intense. As soon as the six Marines were aboard, the crew chief shouted "Take Off!" As the pilot lifted off, the crew chief again came up on the ICS and reported that the team leader had just informed him that two Marines were left in the zone—two Marines who had provided protective fire for the others who boarded the aircraft. The team leader urged the pilot to go back to get them.[15]

The helicopter pilot faced a moral dilemma. The choices were obvious: return to the landing zone to rescue the Marines and risk everything or leave them but save the aircraft, crew, and the six rescued Marines. The pilot had to weigh his responsibilities to the crew against his responsibilities to fellow Marines left in the landing zone. His choice would be conditioned by values and attitudes absorbed in training. They would be difficult, and they would be his alone.

Ethical decisionmaking occurs every time a Marine is faced with a need to decide—now—what to do. It may be a cut-and-dried decision in garrison or it may be one on the battlefield that is far more ambiguous like the one facing the helicopter pilot. At the heart of the leader's ability to choose correctly is a firm grounding in both institutional and individual values that will point the correct direction, even when the Marine is tired or acting under conditions of extreme stress.

These ethical guidelines offer all Marines a proven set of standards by which all Marine actions—or inactions—may be judged.

A professional soldier must be prepared "to rapidly sift through situations and prescribe certain ethical and moral limits to actions which he will tolerate—decisions required . . . under the most trying of times. Simply because we bear arms and wield awesome power, we do not have limitless authority to unleash it without due requirement." We may not say, as one enemy commander said, " 'Kill all, Burn all, Destroy all.' "[16]

Marine leaders must make difficult choices in peacetime, too. At times, these choices will place them in an unfavorable light with either subordinates or higher authority. Regardless of the circumstances, all Marines are expected to choose and to be accountable for their choice.

It was standing operating procedure in Company A to award a 72-hour liberty to platoons which went 30 days with no disciplinary problems. Returning from a lengthy field training period, the 1st Platoon reached 28 days with no problems, only to have a Marine go UA on the 29th. No one outside the platoon knew he was missing. The platoon commander faced a moral dilemma: ignore the UA and ensure his Marines went on a well-earned liberty; or report the absence and forfeit liberty and, perhaps, the morale of his platoon. The platoon commander chose the latter and reported the UA to his company commander. The Marines were disappointed—not only at the loss of hard-earned liberty, but also, initially, in their leader. But slowly, over succeeding days, they came to respect the difficult choice made by the platoon commander. Soon, they came to realize that they were led by a leader who could be counted on to do what was right, no matter how difficult or unpopular. Moreover, the company commander realized he had a subordinate he could trust.

It is not possible to anticipate every circumstance that a leader will face either in combat or in garrison. Corporal Barrett faced a unique set of circumstances and so did the Platoon Commander of the 1st Platoon. It is neither possible to hand down a set of rules that will answer every question, nor is it possible to publish a code that will satisfy every demand. What *is* possible is the establishment of a simple test:

"If you are prepared to talk about your actions, or lack thereof, in front of a national audience, made up of all your seniors, peers, subordinates, and friends who share the same professional values, and whose opinions you value, then your behavior was, or is, probably ethical in nature.[1]"

While the test itself is straightforward, the answers are not. Giving the right answers, and more importantly, doing the right things, requires courage.

## INDIVIDUAL COURAGE

Courage can be misunderstood.[18] It is more than the ability "to overcome the jitters, to quell fear, to conquer the desire to run." [19] It is the ability to know what is, or is not, to be feared. An infantryman charging a bunker is not hampered by the fear that he may be struck down a few paces from his fighting hole. A pilot is not afraid of losing all hydraulic power in his aircraft. They are prepared for those outcomes. A Marine in battle fears disgracing himself by running. He fears not "losing his life, but losing his honor. He may not be able to preserve his life, but he can always preserve his honor. That much is within his power. . . . To fear disgrace but not death, to fear not duty but dereliction from duty—this is courage. The truly courageous do not live in anxiety from morning to night. They are calm because they *know* who they are."[20]

Marines overcome our natural fear of injury and death and fight for three chief reasons: [21] First, we are well-trained and well-led. Second, we have convictions that will sustain us to the last sacrifice. Third, we fight for one another.

At Tarawa, on November 20, 1943, "the first to disembark from the jeep lighter, First Lieutenant Hawkins unhesitatingly moved forward under heavy enemy fire at the end of the Betio Pier, neutralizing emplacements in coverage of troops assaulting the main beach positions. Fearlessly leading his men on to join the forces fighting desperately to gain a beachhead, he repeatedly risked his life throughout the day and night to direct and lead attacks on pillboxes and installations with grenades and demolitions.

"At dawn on the following day, First Lieutenant Hawkins resumed the dangerous mission of clearing the limited beachhead of Japanese resistance, personally initiating an assault on a hostile position fortified by five enemy machine guns, and crawling forward in the face of withering fire, boldly fired point-blank into the loopholes and completed the destruction with grenades. Refusing to withdraw after being seriously wounded in the chest during this skirmish, First Lieutenant Hawkins steadfastly carried the fight to the enemy, destroying three more pillboxes before he was caught in a burst of Japanese shellfire and mortally wounded.[22]"

Although Hawkins was gone, his scout-sniper platoon continued their deadly work clearing out enemy bunkers. Hawkins had inspired his Marines to carry on without him. They were well-trained, well-led, and believed in each other and their cause. Of Hawkins, the assault commander said, "It's not often that you can credit a first lieutenant with winning a battle, but Hawkins came as near to it as any man could. He was truly an inspiration."

Another leader, the commanding officer of Landing Team 2/8, during the same action, was everywhere, "as cool as ice box lettuce."[23]

"Major 'Jim' Crowe—former enlisted man, Marine Gunner, distinguished rifleman, star football player—was a tower of strength throughout the battle. His trademark red mustache bristling, a combat shotgun cradled in his arm, he exuded confidence and professionalism, qualities sorely needed on Betio that long day. Crowe ordered the coxswain of his LCVP 'put this goddamned boat in!' The boat hit the reef at high speed, sending the Marines sprawling. Quickly recovering, Crowe ordered his men over the sides, then led them through several hundred yards of shallow water, reaching the shore intact only four minutes behind his last wave of LVTs. . . . Crowe, clenching a cigar in his teeth and standing upright, growling at his men, 'Look, the sons of bitches can't hit me. Why do you think they can hit you? Get moving. Go!' Red Beach Three was in capable hands."[34]

There is another kind of physical courage—a quiet courage that affects those all around. It is the kind of calm, physical courage that a leader has when all around is chaos and noise. Lieutenant Hawkins' and Major Crowe's commander at Tarawa had that kind of courage. The 4-day struggle to seize Betio Island reached such levels of ferocity that some wondered whether the Marines were winning or losing.

During the battle, especially the early part when the landing seemed to hang in the balance, Colonel David Shoup, the commanding officer of the 2d Marines, remained resolute. Trying to land, his LCVP was stopped by a reef. He transferred to an LVT which had to make three attempts before being able to land, but not before it was hit by plunging shell fire. Colonel Shoup "sustained a painful shell fragment wound in his leg, but led his small party out of the stricken vehicle and into the dubious shelter of the pier. From this position, standing waist-deep in water, surrounded by thousands of dead fish and dozens of floating bodies, Shoup manned his radio. . .[25]"

"In many ways the battle ashore mirrored the worst trench warfare of World War I: infantry against machine guns. In the first day, Shoup's three battalions all lost about half their men and most of their unit cohesion; two reserve battalions suffered similar losses when their troops tried to wade ashore from the reef through a hail of machine gun fire. Punching against the Japanese pillboxes with flame-throwers, demolition charges, hand grenades, and the fire of a few tanks, the 2d Marines and two 8th Marines battalions held only two shallow enclaves along Betio's northwestern shore at the end of the first day.

"On the second day of the battle, the landing hung in the balance, but by the end of the day it swung toward the Marines. The scene around the island sickened the most hardened veterans. Along the beaches LVTs burned, and dead Marines by the score bobbed in lagoon water turned milky by gunfire-blasted coral dust. Smoke and flames blanketed the island. Ruined small craft, broken supplies, and bodies swept along the reef, swirled around the long pier that ran from the shore toward the reef, and littered the beach. The smell of powder, flame, and burnt flesh reached even the amphibious transports. . . .

***"Bunker by bunker, the eight Marine battalions converged, assisted by tank reinforcements and 10th Marines pack howitzers. By the afternoon of the second day, Shoup reassured [General] Smith that the battle had turned: 'Casualties many; percentage dead not known; combat efficiency: We are winning.' "***[26]

Colonel Shoup's assessment was correct and his calm courage under almost unimaginable conditions inspired seniors and subordinates alike. His quiet calmness radiated throughout the battlefield and brought comfort to those who thought the issue was in doubt.

The Armed Forces unification hearings that followed World War II provided Marines an opportunity to show a different kind of courage off the battlefield—*moral cour- age*—the courage to stand up for what is right and for what one believes.

Interservice quarreling cost the Corps Brigadier General "Red Mike" Edson, holder of the Medal of Honor and two Navy Crosses. The Raider leader, who had served longer overseas in World War II than any other Marine officer, was considered by some to be a candidate for Commandant. He disagreed with the unification of the armed forces and could not support it. Edson wanted to speak about it publicly. To protect the Corps from criticism, *he retired.* He left active duty to pursue a course he believed was right. Edson "demonstrated that everyone had an option, if they only had the courage to pursue it." [27] Some officers believed that the example set by Edson was one of the greatest contributions to the unification deliberations.

Leading in combat is vastly different from leading in peacetime. Anybody can give orders and have them obeyed at a peacetime post or station. There, nothing blocks the way to obedience. The brig, pay reductions, and demotion may be all the incentive necessary to instill good order and discipline. But execution of orders in combat may mean "immediate danger, or even the likelihood of being killed; the Marine needs to know why an order is given and how it is to be executed. Above all, Marines need to feel that the leader giving the order knows what he or she is about.[28]

Even given the best training, how Marines perform will depend on the kind of leadership they have, by the example and courage demonstrated by their leader. Napoleon said, "There are no bad regiments, only bad colonels." A unit led by an able and aggressive leader who commands respect because he set the example and demonstrated courage and confidence will perform any task asked of them.[29]

## UNIT ESPRIT

*Esprit de corps*, then, depends on good leadership primarily, but there are other factors. The term implies not only respect between officers and enlisted Marines, but also "a feeling of confidence and comradeship" among the Marines themselves.[30] It refers to the mental and emotional state of the entire unit. It is the spirit that motivates Marines to overcome seemingly insurmountable obstacles. "Each Marine feels the others have good fighting mettle; they will not let one another down. . . . And it means the Marines have pride in their achievements and their reputation as fighters—traditions which must be lived up to." [31] Nowhere else were unit esprit and fighting spirit better demonstrated than in the actions of the 1st Marine Division in November and December 1950.

"Ordered to withdraw . . . in the face of tremendous pressure in the Chosin Reservoir area, the Division began an epic battle against the bulk of the enemy Third Route Army and, while small intermediate garrisons . . . held firmly against repeated and determined attacks by hostile forces, gallantly fought its way successively to Hagaru-ri, Koto-ri, Chinhung-ni, and Hamhung over twisting, mountainous, and icy roads in sub-zero temperatures.

"Battling desperately night and day in the face of almost insurmountable odds throughout a period of two weeks of intense and sustained combat, the First Marine Division, Reinforced, emerged from its ordeal as a fighting unit with its wounded, with its guns and equipment and with its prisoners, decisively defeating seven enemy divisions, together with elements of three others, and inflicting major losses which seriously impaired the military effectiveness of the hostile forces for a considerable period of time. The valiant fighting spirit, relentless perseverance and heroic fortitude of the officers and men of the First Marine Division, Reinforced, in battle against a vastly outnumbering enemy, were in keeping with the highest traditions of the United States Naval Service."[32]

One observer from President Truman's White House, an Army major general, reported that "the Marine Corps was everything it claimed as a force in readiness. 'The First Marine Division is the most efficient and courageous combat unit I have ever seen or heard of.'"[33]

## Being Ready

Our approach to leading is simple, yet unique. It has been carefully tailored to the demands of an expeditionary force in readiness that must be capable, on a moment's notice, of deploying literally anywhere and doing whatever must be done upon arrival—attacking, protecting, or assisting. Many times, decisions will have to be made in the rain, under the partial protection of a poncho, in the drizzle of an uncertain dawn, and without all the facts. At times like that, it will not always be possible to identify all the components of the problem, and use a lengthy and logical problem-solving process to reach a decision. In combat, the decision often must be immediate, and it might have to be instinctive.

It is the Marine Corps' responsibility to prepare leaders of all grades for this moment which will inevitably come. It is the individual Marine's responsibility to overcome the challenges of leading Marines.

A Marine corporal described it this way:

"If effective leadership is evident and functioning, we are strong and ready. If we are well disciplined, of high morale, possess an unquenchable unit spirit, and are efficient, we are the best in the business.

"Strive to create discipline in yourself and your Marines. Encourage high morale, foster esprit, and train for efficiency. You may never win the Medal of Honor, you may never be cited for your outstanding example, but you will have an inner satisfaction that comes only to those that give their all. Then, if you listen carefully . . . you will hear the voices of all the other good Marines who have gone before whisper the greatest commendation of them all—'Well done, Marine.'[34]"

# Chapter 3

# Challenges

*"An army that maintains its cohesion under the most murderous fire; that cannot be shaken by imaginary fears and resists well-founded ones with all its might; that, proud of its victories, will not lose the strength to obey orders and its respect and trust for its officers even in defeat; whose physical power, like the muscles of an athlete, has been steeled by training in privation and effort; a force that regards such efforts as a means to victory rather than a curse on its cause; that is mindful of all these duties and qualities by virtue of the single powerful idea of the honor of its arms—such an army is imbued with the true military spirit."*[1]

—Carl von Clausewitz

## FRICTION

*"Everything in war is very simple, but the simplest thing is difficult. The difficulties accumulate and end by producing a kind of friction that is inconceivable unless one has experienced war."* [2]

Friction dominates war. It makes simple tasks hard, acts constantly to tear down the will of the individual Marine, and interferes with unit cohesion. It operates across the entire spectrum of conflict, from garrison activities to combat, and from Marine air-ground task force command elements down to the most forward fighting position. Friction can be caused by external factors such as the physical environment, the nature of the mission, or friendly or enemy action. Inadequate or inaccurate intelligence also contributes to friction by causing uncertainty. This uncertainty is sometimes called the "fog of war," where things are not always what the leader expected. "This expression describes both the literal fog created by the dust, smoke, and debris of the battlefield, and more importantly the mental fog of confusion and uncertainty created by lack of knowledge of the enemy, the chaotic noise, mental and physical fatigue, and fear."[3]

Friction's most lethal form, however, is self-induced and may be termed internal friction. Fear of the unknown breeds this paralysis. It is best overcome by vigorous leadership, which clearly sets out *what* is happening, *how* it is happening, and, most importantly *why* it is happening.

"Countless minor incidents—the kind you can never really foresee—combine to lower the general level of performance, so that one always falls far short of the intended goal. Iron willpower can overcome this friction; it pulverizes every obstacle, but of course it wears down the machine as well."[4] As FMFM 1 states, "Whatever form it takes, because war is a human enterprise, friction will always have a psychological as well as a physical impact."[5]

The 1975 Cambodian seizure of the unarmed American container ship *Mayaguez*, and its subsequent recapture, is a classic example of what friction can do to leaders at all levels, and its ultimate impact on ground forces.

The operation to recapture the crew and ship began with a sound plan based on the best available intelligence of enemy location, strength, disposition, and intentions. There were no reports of either antiair defenses or of the enemy's intention to significantly resist the rescue. Because there were no Navy and Marine forces on station, the American command- er in Thailand decided to use Air Force helicopters and a Marine battalion flown from Okinawa. The plan called for two Marine assaults; one to board the *Mayaguez*, the other to land on Koh Tang Island where the U. S. crew was thought to be.

"The May 15 boarding of the *Mayaguez* proved anticlimactic, for the Cambodians had abandoned the vessel. But the helo assault on Koh Tang island, where Communists were supposedly holding the crew, became a bloody botch.

"Hoping the Cambodians would see the error of their ways and not resist, the helos plunged in without prior air strikes. Immediately two helos crashed in flames with Marines aboard, and another plunged into the sea after dropping its helo team on the island. Scattered in three different LZs, the hundred or so Marines found themselves fighting for their lives against the enraged Cambodians. As the Marines fought the Communists, the crew of the *Mayaguez* returned safely to American custody from another island, which produced such command confusion and indecision that the Marines on Koh Tang did not receive reinforcements for half a day. In the meantime the three groups of Marines fought their way to one another, supported by Air Force fighters and an AC-130 gunship. With the reinforcements . . . the landing team could hold enough of an LZ to allow a relatively safe extraction during the early evening. . . ." [6]

Like most plans, this one began to unravel almost immediately, first in Washington, then in Thailand, and finally, at Koh Tang Island. *External* friction—a combination of enemy action and severe terrain—and *internal* friction—poor coordination, miscommunication, and unclear, complicated plans with complex command relationships—together prevented the execution of the operation as planned.

Friction is inevitable. Marine leaders must accept it, do everything in their power to minimize its effects, and learn to fight effectively in spite of it.

Among the many factors that cause friction, perhaps the moral and physical challenges to leading are the hardest to overcome. Together, they can produce obstacles that may prevent leaders and units from accomplishing their mission. Although they affect us in very different ways, the moral and physical elements cannot be separated. Moral factors play an important role in developing the physical capacity of individuals and of units.

## Moral Challenge

*"Armies of superior numbers have been put to flight before one man out of ten has fallen. They were not beaten by blows which became more than flesh could bear. They were beaten in spirit according to laws as old as the human heart, and the victor is the one who can best apply those laws."*

When Marines "are moral, the moral power that binds them together and fits them for action is given its main chance for success. There should, therefore, be no confusion about how the word is being used. We are speaking both of training in morals for everyday living and of moral training that will harden the will of a fighting body. One moment's reflection will show why they need not be considered separately. . . . When people conduct lives built on high moral standards and physical fitness, they tend to develop qualities that produce inspired leadership and discipline. It is not a new notion; it can be found in any great military force in the past.[8]"

A battlefield is the place where moral advantage is paramount. Moral ascendancy is an imperative that serves as a primary means of getting the opponent to surrender his will to resist. Gaining moral ascendancy requires that subordinates feel that their leaders genuinely care for them, that they are fighting for a worthy cause and ensuring that their sacrifices are not made in vain. Trust in the Marine Corps and in unit leaders who consistently set the example expected of military professionals is vital to establishing unit cohesion.

Acting as a *buffer* to protect subordinates is a key responsibility of any leader. Leaders must avoid "passing the buck." Leaders must, if necessary, act from the courage of their own convictions, even when such a position runs counter to the policy of seniors. Leaders must always accept full responsibility for their actions, as did the Commanding General, 1st Marine Division, in Korea.

After the success of the Inchon landing and with high hopes of "being home by Christmas," General MacArthur pressed his troops for a knockout blow. Units throughout Korea were pushed north. On November 11th, X Corps with the 1st

Marine Division was ordered to advance all the way to the North Korean-Chinese border. In three separate columns unable to provide mutual support, X Corps advanced north through rugged and difficult terrain. It quickly became a "headlong rush" and the commanding general of the Marine division was worried. His units had become strung out and spread along a single mountain road. He "feared his Marines were out on a limb. With the Eighth Army already thrown back in the west, his left flank was wide open. On November 15, he wrote the Commandant: 'I believe a winter campaign in the mountains of North Korea is too much to ask . . . I doubt the feasibility of supplying troops in this area during the winter or providing for the evacuation of sick and wounded.' . . . The temperature was 4° below zero. . . . [The commanding general] 'deliberately slowed' the Marine advance at Hagaru; his caution would 'prove the division's salvation in the weeks ahead.' "[9]

He and his regimental commanders "were now highly dubious of what might lie ahead of them in the mysterious north. Deliberately, the Marines slowed their advance, even though [the X Corps commander] fretted at their lack of prog- ress. The Marines felt that, strung out as they must be in such terrain, a pellmell rush to the Yalu was highly dangerous. . . . Under . . . prodding, X Corps, including the reluctant, exposed Marines, pushed on." [10] The division commander continued to express his concerns to the corps commander.

The Marine commander "who had no confidence in [the] strategy . . . moved [his] regiments cautiously up the road toward Chosin and paid particular attention to his logistical arrangements and security force . . . along the main supply route (MSR). The weather on November 11 turned miserable. The temperature fell from 32° to -8°, with gusting winds making the cold even more devastating. Provided with only about three-quarters of the cold weather clothing his division required, [the general] ordered the protective clothes distributed to his combat units, but the first cold wave stupefied the troops. With its left flank unprotected . . . and with only scattered . . . units to its right, the division edged up the MSR. [The commanding general] and his staff deflected X Corps demands for more speed and nursed their gnawing suspicion that the 1st Marine Division faced a new war.[1]"

The moral courage of leaders is the key to keeping effective combat units from becoming armed mobs. *Moral courage is a private courage, a form of conscience that can often be an even tougher challenge than physical courage, especially in peacetime.* It serves not only as a foundation of our leadership philosophy; it is also a challenge that Marine leaders must face everyday. If Marines do not have the moral courage in peacetime to meet consistently the high standards and expectations of the Marine Corps, then they are not likely to have the moral courage to make the difficult decisions that may determine the outcome of a battle or a campaign.

## PHYSICAL CHALLENGE

The physical demands of battle encompass more than being fit, and these demands influence both the leader and the led. The effects of sleep deprivation, poor diet, poor hygiene, and most importantly, fear, have to be understood and be a part of everyday training. No one is immune to fatigue. As Marines become increasingly tired, they may lose the ability to make rapid decisions and are susceptible to being confused, disoriented, and ultimately ineffective. "Guts" and "pride" are not a substitute for fitness. A leader relying on "guts" and "pride" will not be able to concentrate fully on the mission or task at hand.

Exact limits of endurance cannot be determined, but physical conditioning is one method of reducing the effects of physical exertion, and it can increase individual self-confidence and reduce stress. The physical development of Marine leaders must include dealing with the natural fear of interpersonal violence, which contributes significantly to the fog and friction of combat. Units, and their leaders, that do not have the mental and physical strength to overcome fear will not be able to fight effectively and overcome friction. In fact, one of the greatest sources of friction is physical exertion, and it may be required of individuals, units, or both. Captain John Ripley's actions in Vietnam vividly depict the physical demands sometimes placed on individuals.

"A rapidly moving, mechanized, North Vietnamese army force, estimated at reinforced divisional strength, was attacking south. . . . It became imperative that a vital river bridge be destroyed if the overall security of the northern provinces of Military Region ONE was to be maintained. Advancing to the bridge to personally supervise this most dangerous but vitally important assignment, Captain Ripley located a large amount of explosives which had been prepositioned there earlier, access to which was blocked by a chain-link fence. In order to reposition the approximately 500 pounds of explosives, Captain Ripley was obliged to reach up and hand-walk along the beams while his body dangled beneath the bridge. On five separate occasions, in the face of constant enemy fire, he moved to points along the bridge and, with the aid of another advisor who pushed the explosives to him, securely emplaced them. He then detonated the charges and destroyed the bridge, thereby stopping the enemy assault."[12]

A commander, fighting his battalion over 4 days of intense combat on Iwo Jima, demonstrated again the physical stamina required of leaders under stress.

"Under a furious barrage of enemy machine-gun and small-arms fire from the commanding cliffs on the right, Colonel Chambers . . . landed immediately after the initial assault waves of his Battalion on D-Day to find the momentum of the assault threatened by heavy casualties from withering Japanese artillery, mortar, rocket, machine-gun and rifle fire. Exposed to relentless hostile fire, he coolly reorganized his battle-weary men, inspiring them to heroic efforts by his own valor and leading them in an attack on the critical, impregnable high ground from which the enemy was pouring an increasing volume of fire directly onto troops ashore as well as amphibious craft in succeeding waves.

"Constantly in the front line encouraging his men to push forward against the enemy's savage resistance, Colonel Chambers led the 8-hour battle to carry the flanking ridge top and reduce the enemy's fields of aimed fire, thus protecting the vital foot-hold gained. In constant defiance of hostile fire while reconnoitering the entire Regimental Combat Team zone of action, he maintained contact with adjacent units and forwarded vital information to the Regimental Commander.

"His zealous fighting spirit undiminished despite terrific casualties and the loss of most of his key officers, he again reorganized his troops for renewed attack against the enemy's main line of resistance and was directing the fire of the rocket platoon when he fell, critically wounded. Evacuated under heavy Japanese fire, Colonel Chambers, by forceful leadership, courage and fortitude in the face of staggering odds, was directly instrumental in insuring the success of subsequent operations of the Fifth Amphibious Corps on Iwo Jima.[13]"

Not every Marine will face the same individual challenge as Captain Ripley, and not every Marine will lead an assault like Colonel Chambers, *but some will.* Marine leaders understand this and work continuously to improve the conditioning of the

Marines under their charge. Part of the leader's job "is to ensure that members of his or her command have every survival edge that can be provided. If people lack the coordinated response that comes only from long, varied and rigorous exercise, they will lack cohesion in action, have much higher combat losses and uselessly expend much of their initial velocity. . . . The gain in moral force deriving from all forms of physical training is an unconscious gain. Will power, determination, mental poise and muscle control all march hand in hand with the general health and well-being of the individual."

Friction and its elements of moral and physical challenges are perhaps the most difficult obstacles to effective leading. How Marines overcome these obstacles, and others not addressed in this manual, is part of our heritage, passed down from our predecessors.

## Overcoming Challenges

*"Assure that all members of the command are acquainted with procedures. . . . ensure the free approach by subordinates for advice and assistance. . . ."*

— Paragraph 1100, *Marine Corps Manual*

## ADAPTABILITY

Adaptability has long been our key to overcoming the effects of friction and its components. Although it is synonymous with flexibility, adaptability also embraces the spirit of innovation. Marines constantly seek to adapt new tactics, organization, and procedures to the realities of the environment. Deficiencies in existing practices are identified, outdated structure discarded, and modifications made to maintain function and utility. The ability to adapt enables Marines to be comfortable within an environment dominated by friction. Experience, common sense, and the critical application of judgment all help Marine leaders persevere.

Marine leaders are the most adaptive of any in the world. Their expeditionary ethos builds in them an ability beyond simply "leaving here," "going there," and "executing set-piece missions." Marine leaders are trained to go forward and adapt to situations, circumstances, and missions not known when they deployed.

One Marine leader said, "Most often, the ingredients of victory are initiative, resourcefulness, adroitness, and improvisation." [15] That is another way of describing adaptability, long a way of life for Marines. More than adapting to changing weather conditions or being able to fight across any type of terrain, the Marine Corps' tradition of adaptability means "getting things done." It means a willingness to deviate from the normal, accepted practices—even from doctrine—if that is what it takes.

During Operation Desert Shield, as Marine forces began to expand their lodgment, one of the "greatest concerns was overland transportation. Doctrinally, the Marine Corps planned for moving support no more than about 50-80 kilometers from a beachhead port. Faced with double and triple these distances, . . . [Marine logistic leaders] resorted to a series of practical if somewhat unconventional actions to solve the problem." By leasing as many civilian trucks as possible, virtually every truck in Saudi Arabia was thrown into some kind of use regardless of its age or mechanical condition. Dubbed "Saudi Motors," the new transport fleet grew to more than 1,400 vehicles and eventually included 50 colorfully decorated 10-ton lorries, over 200 civilian buses, and about 100 rental cars—everything from Toyota Landcruisers, to Mitsubishis, to Jeep Cherokees donated from allied governments.[16]

It was this fleet, together with some quick thinking by Marine leaders that led to the establishment of a remote logistics base well beyond the distances "allowed" by Marine logistics doctrine. A change in tactics by the ground maneuver forces required logisticians to move the main combat service support area along secure but unimproved main supply routes.

"In addition, there were no airfields in the area for casu- alty evacuation or aerial resupply." Situated 170 kilometers and 355 kilometers from the ports of Mishab and Jubayl respectively, the logistics base, dubbed "Al Khanjar" (Arabic for a type of short sword), was built from the desert floor in 14 days. When it was finished, it "included 38 kilometers of blastwall berm which contained among other things the Marine Corps' largest-ever ammunition supply point, 151 cells in 768 acres, a five-million-gallon fuel farm, and a naval hospital with 14 operating rooms. The complex also included two 5,700-foot dirt airstrips capable of handling C-130 turboprop transports."[17]

The ability to improvise is a key characteristic of our Corps. In this case, the piecing together of hundreds of pieces of mismatched equipment, moving it over "impossible" distances, and building a city in the desert literally turned dreams into reality. The ability to find a way—any way—to accomplish the mission is a hallmark of the Corps. All Marines should cherish it, nurture it, and believe in it.

## INNOVATION

Innovation has always been a key component of Marine Corps tradition and our style of leadership. It has come naturally because our "combatant function was and is unique." [18] From the development of dive bombing in Nicaragua, through the pioneering of amphibious warfare between World Wars I and II, to operational maneuver from the sea, Marines have always sought fresh and decisive approaches to problems. Innovation requires that leaders listen to their subordinates and that a two-way system of communication is maintained. Corporals, sergeants, captains, and generals all have the responsibility to be innovators.

Nowhere is our ability to innovate better demonstrated than in the development of our integrated air-ground combat team. The history of Marine aviation since its inception in

1912 is a story of heroism, skill, dedication, and of continuous effort to develop better ways for air and ground forces to operate together. In aviation alone, Marines pioneered the development of close air support, heliborne operations, movable expeditionary airfields, dedicated airborne electronic warfare platforms, vertical/short takeoff and landing jets, expeditionary maintenance organizations and expeditionary, interoperable air command and control systems.

"Sharing the perils and thrills of flying biplanes with their Army and Navy comrades, Marine pilots had the added

advantage of actual combat operations in Haiti, the Dominican Republic, and Nicaragua, which they used to de- velop techniques for supporting ground troops. Among those techniques was dive-bombing, first attempted by Lieutenant L. H. M. Sanderson in 1919, which may be a unique Marine contribution to aerial warfare."[19]

Our reputation as innovators stems, in part, from periodic examinations of our role in the national defense structure. After World War I, our predecessors sought to redefine the Corps which had fought alongside the Army in the trenches in France. They focused on the requirement to seize advanced naval bases and developed doctrine for amphibious operations at a time when the other militaries of the world ignored it as—in the aftermath of Gallipoli—an impossible mission. As Marines became experts in amphibious operations, they also trained U. S. Army divisions in the tactics that would be used by them to land at, among other places, Casablanca, Sicily, Anzio, and Omaha Beach in the European theater; and at Kwajalein, Leyte, and Okinawa in the Pacific.[20] Marines went further still and developed a landing craft and a reef-crossing tractor that became primary tools in both the Pacific and Atlantic theaters of World War II.

"In the early 1920s, the Marines experimented with a British-designed 'Beetle boat' and a Christie amphibian tractor. . . . In 1936, the Marines tried out five different commercial boats as possible landing craft. They even tested fishing boats and boats seized from rum runners; but all had exposed rudders and propellers, and men had to drop as far as 10 feet into the water.

"The answers started to take shape when Andrew J. Higgins, a New Orleans boat builder, working with the Marine Corps and Navy, modified the shallow-water Eureka boat that he had designed for trappers and oil drillers on the Gulf Coast. In

April 1941, . . . Higgins [was shown] pictures that Captain Victor H. Krulak had taken of landing boats the Japanese used at Shanghai in 1937. One type had a ramp in its bow. At his own expense, Higgins put a retractable bow ramp on his 36-foot Eureka boat; this became the precursor of the LCVP of World War II."[21]

"After World War II, General Alexander A. Vandegrift summed up the importance of what the Marine Corps had achieved: 'Despite its outstanding record as a combat force in the past war, the Marine Corps' far greater contribution to victory was doctrinal: that is, the fact that the basic amphibious doctrines which carried Allied troops over every beachhead of World War II had been largely shaped—often in the face of uninterested and doubting military orthodoxy—by U.S. Marines, and mainly between 1922 and 1935.'[23]"

In the 1980's, Marines responded to the challenge of rapidly getting ground forces to the Middle East by creating maritime prepositioning equipment and doctrine. And six decades ago, the Corps codified its vast experience in operations other than war in the *Small Wars Manual*—a manual that is proving its continuing relevance in the emerging security environment of the latter part of the 20th century.[23]

The innovation of Marine leaders has changed the character of war. Whether it was leaders developing a system to use naval gunfire in support of landing forces, studying the art of dive bombing, figuring out how to drop bombs in the dark and in all kinds of weather, or developing and proving the concept of maritime prepositioning, they all demonstrated the impact of Marine leaders who combined vision and *initiative.*

***"The essence of loyalty is the courage to propose the unpopular, coupled with a determination to obey, no matter how distasteful the ultimate decision. And the essence of leadership is the ability to inspire such behavior."***[24]

One Marine leader developed a set of "rules" he followed to promote innovation and creativity.[25] First, leaders should make it their duty to bring subordinates' ideas and criticisms to the surface where all may analyze and evaluate them. Ask for ideas and you will get them. Second, leaders must clear a path to their doorstep. Subordinates should use the chain of command, but ideas must rise to the top. Leaders must allow subordinates the opportunity to show initiative. Third, because innovation is imprecise and because subordinates, especially junior ones, will make mistakes, protect them. "Zero defects" are not a standard of measurement. They do not encourage initiative; they stifle it. Lastly, emphasize that you expect honest expression of the subordinate's best thinking. Do not tolerate patronizing behavior.

***"If we wish to think clearly, we must cease imitating; if we wish to cease imitating, we must make use of our imagination. We must train ourselves for the unexpected in place of training others for the cut and dried. Audacity, and not caution, must be our watchword."***[26]

## DECENTRALIZATION

Decentralization is simply authorizing subordinates to act, guided by commander's intent and focus of effort, in situations where judgment and experience dictate action. The one concept that is repeated again and again within classic military literature is the advantage of allowing junior leaders to apply judgment and act upon their decisions. The Marine Corps has always enjoyed great success decentralizing au- thority to the lowest levels. Marines fighting expeditionary wars during the first half of this century exemplified this. Whether on duty in the Legation Quarter in China during the 1920's, with the Gendarmerie in Haiti, or on patrol with the Guardia in Nicaragua, junior Marines—sergeants and lieutenants—helped enforce United States policy, kept law and order, suppressed revolts against governments, and protected American lives, interests, and property.

During World War II, the actions of junior leaders were directly responsible for our successes in the island campaigns of the Pacific. Decentralized decisionmaking—pushing authority, responsibility, and accountability to the lowest levels—promoted speed in execution. In battle after battle, small units were able to make a decisive difference because of the actions of subordinate leaders. Of Tarawa, Colonel Merritt A. Edson mentioned decentralization and adaptability as important parts of the final outcome. "It is my opinion that the reason we won this show was the ability of the junior officers and noncoms to take command of small groups of six to eight or ten men, regardless of where these men came from, and to organize and lead them as a fighting team.[27]

As a result of these experiences, the Marine Corps developed the modern-day fire team and produced the world's finest noncommissioned officers. The tradition of encouraging decentralized decisionmaking continues today and is manifested in such peacetime duty as that performed by Marine Security Guard detachments commanded by staff noncommissioned officers, drill instructors at recruit depots and Officer Candidates School, and the small-unit combat patrols in the strife-torn streets of every corner of the globe.

Testimony to the skills of Marine small-unit leaders was the development of the combined action program (CAP). First used with success in Haiti (1915-1934), Nicaragua (1926-1933), and in Santo Domingo (1916-1922), it was used again in Vietnam.[28] There, the combined force was commanded by a Marine squad leader—a sergeant or a corporal—and demonstrated the positive benefits of decentralization.

"In principle, the CAP was simplicity itself. In execution, it demanded political and tactical sophistication. The program required that a specially selected and trained Marine rifle squad join a Popular Forces (militia) platoon and work in concert to provide continuous security from the VC. The Marines would live and work among the people and inspire the PF to conduct night-time patrols and ambushes.[29]

Decentralization was at the heart of the CAP program. Its success lay in a tradition of Marine leadership: the encouragement of subordinates. Give subordinates all the initiative and latitude they can handle by decentralizing authority. "Tell them what results you want, and leave the 'how' to them.[30]"

"Make it clear what you want done and who is to do it. . . . Remember the old promotion-examination question for lieutenants, in which the student is told that he has a ten-man working party, headed by a sergeant, and must erect a 75-foot flagpole. . . . Problem—How to do it?

"Every student who works out the precise calculations of stresses, tackle, and gear, no matter how accurately, is graded wrong. The desired answer is simple: The lieutenant turns to the sergeant, and says, 'Sergeant, put up that flagpole.[31]'"

## Will

All leaders—even the most famous—lead in much the same way, at least partially, because they *think* in much the same way, "in terms of intuitions, fears, guilts, and occasional flashes of reasoned insight." [32] Why then, do some Marine leaders succeed and others fail? What is it that some leaders have that others do not? What all successful leaders have in common is a strength of will that enables them to face the most challenging of tasks and extract the most from their subordinates. Captain William Barber's performance from 28 November to 2 December 1950 demonstrates the importance of a leader's will.

"Assigned to defend a three-mile mountain pass along the division's main supply line and commanding the only route of approach in the march from Yudam-ni to Hagaru-ri, Captain Barber took position with his battle weary troops and, before nightfall, had dug in and set up a defense along the frozen, snow-covered hillside. When a force of estimated regimental strength savagely attacked during the night, inflicting heavy casualties and finally surrounding his position following a bitterly fought seven-hour conflict, Captain Barber, after repulsing the enemy, gave assurance that he could hold if supplied by air drops and requested permission to stand fast when orders were received . . . to fight his way back to a relieving force after two reinforcing units had been driven back under fierce resistance in their attempts to reach the isolated troops.

"Aware that leaving the position would sever contact with the 8,000 Marines trapped at Yudam-ni and jeopardize their chances of joining the 3,000 more awaiting their arrival at Hagaru-ri for the continued drive to the sea, he chose to risk loss of his command rather than sacrifice more men if the enemy seized control and forced a renewed battle to regain the position, or abandon his many wounded who were unable to walk.

"Although severely wounded . . . Captain Barber continued to maintain personal control, often moving up and down the lines on a stretcher to direct the defense and consistently encouraging and inspiring his men to supreme efforts despite the staggering opposition. Waging desperate battle throughout five days and six nights of repeated on-slaughts launched by the fanatical aggressors, he and his heroic command accounted for approximately 1,000 enemy dead in this epic stand in bitter sub-zero weather, and when the company was relieved, only 82 of his original 220 men were able to walk away from the position so valiantly defended against insuperable odds. His profound faith and courage, great personal valor and unwavering fortitude were decisive factors in the successful withdrawal of the division from the deathtrap in the Chosin Reservoir sector. . . .[36]

It was tough-minded leaders like Captain Barber and Lieutenant Colonel Ray Murray that held units together under

extreme stress. Lieutenant Colonel Murray, commanding the 5th Marines at the Chosin Reservoir, summed up what was required of leaders: "I personally felt in a state of shock, the kind of shock one gets from some great personal tragedy, the sudden loss of someone close. . . . My first fight was within myself. I had to rebuild that emptiness of spirit."[34]

For leaders to hold units together under adverse conditions, they must first fight—and win—the battle within themselves.

## FIGHTING POWER AND WINNING

Fighting power is an organization's ability to conduct combat operations by overcoming challenges to lead, compete, and prevail on the battlefield. Creating and sustaining superior fighting power requires the combination of the tangible ac- tivities of war—maneuver, firepower, and protection—with the intangible elements of war—leadership, unit esprit, and individual courage. According to one historian, fighting power "rests on mental, intellectual, and organizational foun- dations; its manifestations, in one combination or another, are discipline and cohesion, morale and initiative, courage and toughness, the willingness to fight and the readiness, if necessary, to die. 'Fighting Power,' in brief, is defined as the sum total of mental qualities that make armies fight."[35]

Fighting power is what took the 2d Marine Division over the seawall at Tarawa, into the face of prepared defenses and devastating fire; it is what kept the "flying leathernecks" of the "Cactus Air Force" on Guadalcanal launching again and again from the shell-pocked runway of Henderson Field; it is what brought the 1st Marine Division down intact from the Chosin Reservoir to the sea; and it was what three under-strength Marine battalions used to help recapture the Citadel in Hue City.

Fighting power is what makes certain units superior to others on the battlefield; it enables organizations to sustain high casualties and continue their missions, and it can compensate for material deficiencies. *Fighting power remains the ultimate measure of all military leadership effectiveness*

For more than two centuries Marines have produced victory. It has been the vitality of the Marine leader that has upheld the "critical foundations of our Corps in the searing cauldron of combat." Whatever the challenges, Marines have overcome them using the foundations of Marine Corps leadership—foundations steeped in the values, traditions, customs, and history of our Corps. It is a unique blend of ethos and standards not found anywhere else in the world and is more than simple obedience to orders. Leading Marines is more than just a simple awareness of responsibility. It is a commitment and an obligation to those who follow.

# Epilogue

*"The time always comes in battle when the decisions of statesmen and of generals can no longer effect the issue and when it is not within the power of our national wealth to change the balance decisively. Victory is never achieved prior to that point; it can be won only after the battle has been delivered into the hands of men who move in imminent danger of death."*[1]

—S.L.A. Marshall

In one of the many fights enroute to Chosin on the hills north of Yudam-ni, a private named Stanley Robinson had taken command of a decimated squad. Later wounded, Robinson lay on a stretcher in a warming tent of the medical battalion and listened "to the cascading sound of a fire fight to the north. It was not long before the ambulance jeeps drew up outside. Litterbearers brought in a stretcher and placed it alongside Robinson.

" 'What outfit you from?' Robinson asked. 'Easy, 7th,' the inert figure mumbled. 'Did we get hit?' 'Clobbered. Mr. Yancey's wounded—so's the skipper—everybody is, I guess.'

"Robinson sat up. In the darkness he got into his clothes and parka. He stifled a moan as he pulled the shoe-pacs on over his swollen feet. 'Be seein' you, Mac,' he whispered. Robinson stumbled to the entrance and lurched through the opening. The cold night air made him gasp. He was selecting a weapon from a discarded stack of rifles when a corpsman came to him.

" 'What'n hell you doin', Robinson?' 'What does it look like, Doc?' . . . Robinson slung the rifle over his shoulder and headed for the hill mass to the north. When he came to the steep hillside he had to crawl. The blisters on his feet had broken and his socks were wet with blood and pus. Robinson found his way to Easy Company, [and] he found Yancey. 'What'n hell you doin' here?' Yancey asked hoarsely. 'Looking for a job.' Yancey spat blood in the snow. 'You got one. Over there.' "[2]

Private Robinson's action in 1950 captured the essence of Marine Corps leadership. Leaving the warming tent, selecting a weapon, and struggling to rejoin his battered platoon was an act of extraordinary personal courage, but it was not an aberration; instead, it was an act that sprang from the rich tradition of Marine leadership manifested in hundreds of battles—from Chapultepec to Blanc Mont Ridge to Okinawa. It is a tradition that continues today in countless ways and in countless places.

Marines understand why there was no emotional greeting from Yancey when Robinson rejoined the platoon. Thanks were neither expected nor given. Both knew he would rejoin the outfit, if he could. They were Marines, with the enemy in their front, and their division decisively engaged. Where else could Robinson be? There was work to be done, serious fighting, and because of the actions of thousands of leaders like Private Robinson—leading teams, squads, and platoons—the outnumbered division prevailed.

Thirty-three years later, an unnamed lance corporal in Beirut asked the same question: "Where else should I be?" These examples, so tightly wound into the concepts of personal example, courage, and unit *esprit* that they cannot be separated, demonstrate the eternal strength of the Marine Corps. For in the final analysis, Marine leaders must be prepared to act alone, when all others choose to sit, or when others find a way to stand aside to let someone else take the lead. Marines cannot stand aside because to do so compromises their very self-identity as Marines. Private Robinson understood this. Knowing that his fellow Marines counted on him, Robinson acted in the only way he could.

One can always imagine situations in combat when the choices will be clear and obvious, though not necessarily easy. More difficult, but no less important, is discovering those challenges in peacetime. Preparing for those challenges—what we do in training—shapes directly what we do in combat. In any team sport, teams play the way they practice. Similarly, Marines fight the way they train. While it is easy to give in on the "small things," eventually that surrender may cause the collapse of a "large thing" in combat. The actions of Private Robinson were the natural and logical culmination of his training and the leadership to which he had been exposed. Because it had been severe but fair, hard but rewarding, when he had to decide—alone—what to do, his choice was easy: He rejoined his Marines.

All the rank in the world will not draw a fire team forward unless it has confidence in the Marine who leads it. Marines have a reasonable expectation that their leaders will come up with plans that will accomplish the mission and give them the best possible chance of succeeding. They do not ask for certainty, just the best possible preparation and skills from their leaders. The Marine Corps works hard to train leaders, but *the most important and fundamental leadership training and education must come through self-study and self-examination.*

Marines do not climb from their fighting holes, or leave warming tents, and go forward into fire, the unknown, and possibly even death because of grandiose visions about the national interest, the international security structure, or even love of family or our American culture. They go forward because of their friends and comrades—fellow Marines, who display their special skills and abilities for each other, and often, in the ultimate loneliness of close combat, for each other alone. As was said of Marines in Korea, "These Marines had pride in their service, which had been carefully instilled in them, and they had pride in themselves, because each man had made the grade in a hard occupation. They would not lightly let their comrades down. And they had discipline, which in essence is the ability not to question orders but to carry them out as intelligently as possible.[8]

And we still don't let our comrades down. The risk of death has always been preferable to letting a fellow Marine down. This is expressed in the actions of a rifleman continuing forward in rushes under heavy fire, and in a pilot bring-ing his aircraft around for another attack while the antiair- craft guns continue to seek the range. This is why the word "Marine" has always been synonymous with the very best self-sacrificing leadership our nation produces.

These enduring foundations support more than just our institution. They support individual Marines for the rest of their lives, in service and out. A former Marine described his "foundations" this way:

"My life experience has taught me again and again the value of the time I spent in the Marine Corps. The values I learned and lived while a Marine, the values of self-reliance, self-discipline, honor, courage as well as physical and mental toughness have enabled me to make a success of my life. Moreover, I would add this bit of perspective; the Marine Corps has won many victories for which it is famous. However, the Corps has won many personal and private victories in the hearts and minds of the men and women who have worn the uniform. It has . . . imbued the lives of many common Americans with the necessary character traits to master their own lives and to achieve great things. These many personal victories sometimes go unnoticed but they are meaningful and of great value, in-and-of-themselves, as well as to this Nation."[4]

"It is this continuity of the spirit, purpose, and tradition, these many and intangible forces, which are the strengths that support Marines as they go into harm's way. We are what our institution demands that we be; and our institution is what it is because of these foundations; no more and no less."[5] Marines lead because of the adaptability, innovation, strength of will, and devotion to our Corps learned from our predecessors. They lead, and win, not because of what they may be as individuals, but rather because of what they are as *Marines*.

*"The U. S. Marine Corps has evolved its mystical appeal slowly, through an unusual combination of circumstance, good fortune, and, most of all, conviction in the hearts of resolute men. It is a combination that has both strengthened and brought glory to the United States.*

*"Although the Corps contains its share of visible heroes, its triumphs, in an aberration of history, are triumphs of the institution itself and not the attainments of individual Marines. We remember that Marlborough defeated the French, that Togo defeated the Russians, that Scipio defeated Carthage. But we know only that it was the Marines who won at Belleau Wood, the Marines who won at Guadalcanal, the Marines who led the way at Inchon. And that is exactly the way the Corps's heroes—big and small—would have it, for the Corps is less of the flesh than of the spirit."*[6]

These are the legacies that we have inherited and that we must pass on. *Learn them, study them, and live them.*

***Semper Fidelis . . .***

# Appendices

*Marine Corps Manual*, Paragraph 1100 — Core Values — Leadership Traits — Leadership Principles — The Oaths — Trust

# Marine Corps Manual

## SECTION B—MANAGEMENT

### 1100. MILITARY LEADERSHIP

1. Purpose and Scope

a. The primary goal of Marine Corps leadership is to instill in all Marines the fact that we are warriors first. The only reason the United States of America needs a Marine Corps is to fight and win wars. Everything else is secondary. In North China in 1937, Captain Samuel B. Griffith said, "Wars and battles are not lost by private soldiers. They win them, but don't lose them. They are lost by commanders, staffs, and troop leaders, and they are often lost long before they start." Our leadership training is dedicated to the purpose of preparing those commanders, staffs, and troop leaders to lead our Marines in combat.

b. Marine Corps Leadership qualities include:

(1) Inspiration—Personal example of high moral standards reflecting virtue, honor, patriotism, and subordination in personal behavior and in performance.

(2) Technical proficiency—Knowledge of the military sciences and skill in their application.

(3) Moral responsibility—Personal adherence to high standards of conduct and the guidance of subordinates toward wholesomeness of mind and body.

2. Responsibility

a. The Commandant of the Marine Corps is directly responsible to the Secretary of the Navy for establishing and maintaining leadership standards and conducting leadership training within the Marine Corps.

b. Commanders will ensure that local policies, directives and procedures reflect the special trust and confidence reposed in members of the officer corps. Full credit will be given to their statements and certificates. They will be allowed maximum discretion in the exercise of authority vested in them, and they and their dependents will be accorded all prerogatives and perquisites which are traditional and otherwise appropriate. Except in cases where more stringent positive identification procedures are required for the proper security of classified material and installations, or are imposed by higher authority for protecting privileges reserved for eligible military personnel, the officers' uniforms will amply attest to their status, and their oral statements will serve to identify them and their dependents.

c. An individual's responsibility for leadership is not dependent upon authority. Marines are expected to exert proper influence upon their comrades by setting examples of obedience, courage, zeal, sobriety, neatness, and attention to duty.

d. The special trust and confidence, which is expressly reposed in officers by their commission, is the distinguishing privilege of the officer corps. It is the policy of the Marine Corps that this privilege be tangible and real; it is the corresponding obligation of the officer corps that it be wholly deserved.

(1) As an accompanying condition commanders will impress upon all subordinate officers the fact that the presumption of integrity, good manners, sound judgment, and discretion, which is the basis for the special trust and confidence reposed in each officer, is jeopardized by the slightest transgression on the part of any member of the officer corps. Any offense, however minor, will be dealt with promptly, and with sufficient severity to impress on the officer at fault, and on the officer corps. Dedication to the basic elements of special trust and confidence is a Marine officer's obligation to the officer corps as a whole, and transcends the bonds of personal friendship.

(2) As a further and continuing action, commanders are requested to bring to the attention of higher authority, referencing this paragraph, any situation, policy, directive, or procedure which contravenes the spirit of this paragraph, and which is not susceptible to local correction.

(3) Although this policy is expressly concerned with commissioned officers, its provisions and spirit will, where applicable, be extended to noncommissioned officers, especially staff noncommissioned officers.

3. Personal Relations. Effective personal relations in an organization can be satisfactory only when there is complete understanding and respect between individuals. Commanders must:

a. Strive for forceful and competent leadership throughout the entire organization.

b. Inform the troops of plans of action and reasons therefor, whenever it is possible and practicable to do so.

c. Endeavor to remove on all occasions those causes which make for misunderstanding or dissatisfaction.

d. Assure that all members of the command are acquainted with procedures for registering complaints, together with the action taken thereon.

e. Build a feeling of confidence which will ensure the free approach by subordinates for advice and assistance not only in military matters but for personal problems as well.

4. Relations Between Officers and Enlisted Marines. Duty relationships and social and business contacts among Marines

of different grades will be consistent with traditional standards of good order and discipline and the mutual respect that has always existed between Marines of senior grade and those of lesser grade. Situations that invite or give the appearance of familiarity or undue informality among Marines of different grades will be avoided or, if found to exist, corrected. The following paragraphs written by the then Major General Commandant John A. Lejeune appeared in the Marine Corps Manual, Edition of 1921, and since that time have defined the relationship that will exist between Marine officers and enlisted members of the Corps:

a. "Comradeship and brotherhood.—The World War wrought a great change in the relations between officers and enlisted men in the military services. A spirit of comradeship and brotherhood in arms came into being in the training camps and on the battlefields. This spirit is too fine a thing to be allowed to die. It must be fostered and kept alive and made the moving force in all Marine Corps organizations.

b. "Teacher and scholar.—The relation between officers and enlisted men should in no sense be that of superior and inferior nor that of master and servant, but rather that of teacher and scholar. In fact, it should partake of the nature of the relation between father and son, to the extent that officers, especially commanding officers, are responsible for the physical, mental, and moral welfare, as well as the discipline and military training of the young men under their command who are serving the nation in the Marine Corps.

c. "The realization of this responsibility on the part of officers is vital to the well-being of the Marine Corps. It is especially so, for the reason that so large a proportion of the men enlisting are under twenty-one years of age. These men are in the formative period of their lives, and officers owe it to them, to their parents, and to the nation, that when discharged from the services they should be far better men physically, mentally, and morally than they were when they enlisted.

d. "To accomplish this task successfully a constant effort must be made by all officers to fill each day with useful and interesting instruction and wholesome entertainment for the men. This effort must be intelligent and not perfunctory, the object being not only to do away with idleness, but to train and cultivate the bodies, the minds, and the spirit of our men.

e. "Love of corps and country.—To be more specific, it will be necessary for officers not only to devote their close attention to the many questions affecting the comfort, health, military training and discipline of the men under their command, but also actively to promote athletics and to endeavor to enlist the interest of their men in building up and maintaining their bodies in the finest physical condition; to encourage them to enroll in the Marine Corps Institute and to keep up their studies after enrollment; and to make every effort by means of historical, educational and patriotic address to cultivate in their hearts a deep abiding love of the corps and country.

f. "Leadership.—Finally, it must be kept in mind that the American soldier responds quickly and readily to the exhibition of qualities of leadership on the part of his officers. Some of these qualities are industry, energy, initiative, determination, enthusiasm, firmness, kindness, justness, self-control, unselfishness, honor, and courage. Every officer should endeavor by all means in his power to make himself the possessor of these qualities and thereby to fit himself to be a real leader of men."

5. Noncommissioned Officers. The provisions of paragraphs 1100.3 and 1100.4 above, apply generally to the relationships of noncommissioned officers with their subordinates and apply specifically to noncommissioned officers who may be exercising command authority.

# Core Values

Generation after generation of American men and women have given special meaning to the term United States Marine. They have done so by their performance on and off the battlefield. Feared by enemies, respected by allies, and loved by the American people, Marines are a "special breed." This reputation was gained and is maintained by a set of enduring core values. These values form the cornerstone, the bedrock, and the heart of our character. They are the guiding beliefs and principles that give us strength, influence our attitudes, and regulate our behavior. They bond our Marine family into a total force that can meet any challenge.

**HONOR:** The bedrock of our character. The quality that guides Marines to exemplify the ultimate in ethical and moral behavior; never to lie, cheat, or steal; to abide by an uncompromising code of integrity; to respect human dignity; to have respect and concern for each other. The quality of maturity, dedication, trust, and dependability that commits Marines to act responsibly; to be accountable for actions; to fulfill obligations; and to hold others accountable for their actions.

**COURAGE:** The heart of our core values, courage is the mental, moral, and physical strength ingrained in Marines to carry them through the challenges of combat and the mastery of fear; to do what is right; to adhere to a higher standard of personal conduct; to lead by example, and to make tough decisions under stress and pressure. It is the inner strength that enables a Marine to take that extra step.

**COMMITMENT:** The spirit of determination and dedication within members of a force of arms that leads to professionalism and mastery of the art of war. It leads to the highest order of discipline for unit and self; it is the ingredient that enables 24-hour-a-day dedication to Corps and Country; pride; concern for others; and an unrelenting determination to achieve a standard of excellence in every endeavor. Commitment is the value that establishes the Marine as the warrior and citizen others strive to emulate.

Reaffirm these core values and ensure they guide your performance, behavior, and conduct every minute of every day.

## Leadership Traits

Integrity

Knowledge

Justice

Courage

Enthusiasm

Decisiveness

Bearing

Dependability

Endurance

Initiative

Unselfishness

Tact

Loyalty

Judgment

# Leadership Principles

*Be technically and tactically proficient*

*Know yourself and seek self-improvement*

*Know your Marines and look out for their welfare*

*Keep your Marines informed*

*Set the example*

*Ensure the task is understood, supervised, and accomplished*

*Train your Marines as a team*

*Make sound and timely decisions*

*Develop a sense of responsibility among your subordinates*

*Employ your unit in accordance with its capabilities*

*Seek responsibility, and take responsibility for your actions*

# The Oaths

The oath that accompanies commissionings, enlistments, and promotions should not be taken lightly. While the words are simple, when Marines swear "to support and defend the Constitution of the United States against all enemies, foreign and domestic," they are assuming a most challenging and defining obligation. What a Marine is actually doing is "pledging his means, his talent, his very life, to his country. This is an obligation that falls to very few. . . .[1]"

The oath is one of acceptance. Because it is an oath of consent, taking the oath of allegiance is the pivotal factor which changes the status from that of civilian to that of Marine. After taking the oath, Marines find themselves transformed in a way that cannot be captured in words. It is why Marines long out of uniform bristle at being called "ex-Marines" because they consider themselves to still be Marines.[2]

The oaths appear on page 108.

## Oath of Office

*I, ________________, do solemnly swear (or affirm) that I will support and defend the Constitution of the United States against all enemies, foreign and domestic; that I will bear true faith and allegiance to the same; that I take this obligation freely, without any mental reservation or purpose of evasion; and that I will well and faithfully discharge the duties of the office on which I am about to enter. So help me God.*

## Oath of Enlistment

*I, ________________, do solemnly swear (or affirm) that I will support and defend the Constitution of the United States against all enemies, foreign and domestic; that I will bear true faith and allegiance to the same; and that I will obey the orders of the President of the United States and the orders of the officers appointed over me, according to regulations and the Uniform Code of Military Justice. So help me God.*

# Trust

*To all who shall see these presents, greeting:*

*Know ye that, reposing special trust and confidence in the patriotism, valor, fidelity and abilities of I do.*

With these few short words, Marine leaders are set apart from other American citizens. The special trust granted officers by the President of the United States or to enlisted Marines by the Commandant of the Marine Corps gives leaders certain privileges, but more importantly, subjects them to special responsibilities and obligations. Dedication to the basic elements of special trust and confidence is the Marine leader's obligation to the Marine Corps as a whole, and transcends the bonds of personal friendship.[1]

*To all who shall see these presents, greeting:*

*Know Ye, that reposing special trust and confidence in the fidelity and abilities of I do.*

# Notes

There are hundreds, even thousands, of excellent books, articles, and vignettes on leading. Only a few have been cited in this book, but many others were extremely useful as background material. A study of some of the works cited in this book would be a good starting point for independent research and reading on the art of leading Marines.

Corrections and modifications in quotations have been made where appropriate to condense, to clarify, or to make points clearer. Every effort has been made to keep the essential message of the original. All textual modifications have been indicated in the endnotes.

## Our Ethos

1. T. R. Fehrenbach, *This Kind of War* (New York: Bantam Books, 1991) p. 183 and p. 182.

2. Lieutenant General Victor H. Krulak, USMC (Ret.), *First To Fight: An Inside View of the U.S. Marine Corps* (Annapolis, MD: Naval Institute Press, 1984) p. 155.

3. *Ibid.*

4. Captain John W. Thomason, Jr., USMC, *Fix Bayonets!* (New York: Charles Scribner's Sons, 1927) p. ix.

5. On 25 October 1983, 2 days after the bombing, then Commandant of the Marine Corps, General P. X. Kelley, visited the U. S. Air Force Regional Medical Center in Wiesbaden, Germany, where he met with Lance Corporal Jeffrey Nashton who had been critically injured.

6. This is from remarks by General Robert H. Barrow before the House of Representatives of the Commonwealth of Pennsylvania 2 June 1981.

7. Much of the material in this section "The U.S. Marine" is taken from General Carl E. Mundy, Jr., "What Is It That Makes Marines?," *Marine Corps Gazette* (March 1993) p. 15 unless otherwise noted.

8. Malcolm S. Forbes, "They Know Their Business," *Forbes* (December 1, 1963) p. 33.

9. Thomason, p. xiv.

10. Fehrenbach, p. 168.

11. Colonel Robert Debs Heinl, Jr., USMC, *Soldiers of* (Annapolis, MD: United States Naval Institute, 1962) p. 542.

12. *Ibid,* p. 543.

13. *Ibid,* p. 603.

14. Much of the material in this section "Every Marine a Rifleman" is taken from General Carl E. Mundy, Jr., "Every Marine a Rifleman," *Marine Corps Gazette* (January 1993) pp. 12–13 unless otherwise noted.

15. William Manchester, *Goodbye, Darkness: A Memoir of the Pacific War* (Boston, MA: Little, Brown and Company, 1979) p. 391.

16. Master Sergeant C. V. Crumb, FMCR, "What It Means To Be a Marine," *Marine Corps Gazette* (January 1960) pp. 20–21 with textual changes.

17. Much of the material in this section "Soldiers of the Sea" is taken from General Carl E. Mundy, Jr., "What Is It That Makes Marines?," *Marine Corps Gazette* (March 1993) p. 15 unless otherwise noted.

18. Earl H. Ellis, "713H—Operation Plan, Advanced Base Operations in Micronesia 1921" (Washington D.C.: U. S. Marine Corps Museums, Personal Papers Collection) p. 20.

19. Much of the material in this section "The Marine Tradition" is taken from General Carl E. Mundy, Jr., "What Is It

That Makes Marines?," *Marine Corps Gazette* (March 1993) p. 14 unless otherwise noted.

20. Armed Forces Information Service, *The Armed Forces Officer* (Washington, D.C.: Department of Defense, 1975) pp. 56–57.

21. Krulak, pp. 160–161.

22. Fehrenbach, p. 640.

## Foundations

1. Major General John A. Lejeune, USMC, as quoted in *Marine Corps Manual* Paragraph 1100.4a. See p. 97.

2. U. S. Marine Corps, FMFM 1, *Warfighting* (Washington, D. C.: Headquarters, U. S. Marine Corps, 1989) p. 45.

3. Charles Edmundson, "Why Warriors Fight," *Marine Corps Gazette* (September 1944) p. 3 with minor textual changes.

4. FMFM 1, *Warfighting*, p. 44.

5. U. S. Marine Corps, NAVMC 2767, *User's Guide to Marine Corps Leadership* (Washington, D. C.: Headquarters,

U. S. Marine Corps, 1984) Section 203: Profession of Arms, p. 1.

6. General Sir John Hackett, *The Profession of Arms* (New York: Macmillan Publishing Company, 1983) p. 202.

7. Colonel Robert D. Heinl, Jr., USMC (Ret.), *The Marine Officer's Guide*, 4th ed. (Annapolis, MD: Naval Institute Press, 1977) p. 367.

8. Adapted from Major Guy Richards, "You and Your Troops," *Marine Corps Gazette*(December 1944) p. 30.

9. A letter to General L. F. Chapman, Jr., USMC, as cited in a letter to All General Officers and All Commanding Officers, dated 19 July 1971, with minor textual changes.

10. U. S. Marine Corps, *Marine Corps Manual*, Paragraph 1100.1b(1). See p. 93.

11. Major General John. A. Lejeune, USMC, *The Reminiscences of a Marine* (Philadelphia: Dorrance and Company, 1930: reprint ed., Quantico, VA: Marine Corps Association, 1990) p. 100.

12. Armed Forces Information Service, *The Armed Forces Officer* (Washington, D. C.: Department of Defense, 1975) p. 50.

13. From CMC correspondence files.

14. *The Navy Cross: Vietnam*, edited by Paul D. Stevens (Forest Ranch, CA: Sharp and Dunnigan Publications, Inc., 1989) p. 25.

15 NAVMC 2767, Section 205: Instilling and Developing Values, pp. 12–13 with changes.

16 *Ibid*, Section 206: Ethical Leadership, p. D-4 with minor textual changes.

17 *Ethics for the Junior Officer*, edited by Karel Montor (Annapolis, MD: Naval Institute Press, 1994) p. xv with minor textual changes.

18. Much of the material in this paragraph is taken or adapted from John Silber, "The Ethics of the Sword," remarks made 21 February 1989, The Morse Auditorium, Boston University, Boston, MA.

19. *Ibid*, typescript, p. 21.

20. *Ibid.*

21. Taken and adapted from Charles Edmundson, "Why Warriors Fight," p. 3.

22. *The Congressional Medal of Honor: The Names, The Deeds* (Forest Ranch, CA: Sharp and Dunnigan Publications, Inc., 1984) pp. 341–42 with additional paragraph indentation.

23. Colonel Joseph H. Alexander, USMC (Ret.), *Across the Reef: The Marine Assault of Tarawa* (Washington, D. C.: U. S. Marine Corps Historical Center, 1993) p. 25.

24. *Ibid,* p. 15.

25. *Ibid,* p. 17.

26. Allan R. Millett, *Semper Fidelis: The Story of the United States Marine Corps* (New York: Macmillan Publishing Company, 1980) pp. 397–398.

27. Jon T. Hoffman, *Once A Legend* (Novato, CA: Presidio Press, 1994) pp. 379–380.

28. Edmundson, p. 8 with minor textual changes.

29. *Ibid,* with minor textual changes.

30. *Ibid,* p. 9.

31. *Ibid,* with minor textual changes.

32. Jane Blakeney, *Heroes: U. S. Marine Corps 1861-1953 — Armed Forces Awards-Flags*, "First Marine Division, Reinforced" (1957) p. 362.

33. Millett, p. 498.

34. Corporal Gary C. Cooper, "Guideposts to Leadership," *Marine Corps Gazette* (July 1960) p. 35 with minor textual changes.

## Challenges

1. Carl von Clausewitz, *On War*, translated and edited by Michael Howard and Peter Paret (Princeton, NJ: Princeton University Press, 1989) pp. 187–188.

2. *Ibid*, p. 119.

3. NAVMC 2767, *User's Guide to Marine Corps Leadership* (Washington, D.C.: U. S. Marine Corps, 1984) Section 217: Combat Leadership, p. 12.

4. Clausewitz, p. 119.

5. U. S. Marine Corps, FMFM 1, *Warfighting* (Washington, D.C.: Headquarters, U. S. Marine Corps, 1989) p. 5.

6. Allan R. Millett, *Semper Fidelis: The History of the United States Marine Corps* (New York: Macmillan

Publishing Company, 1980) pp. 605–606 with additional paragraph indentation.

7. Lynn Montross, *War Through the Ages* (New York: Harper & Brothers, 1946) p. 36.

8. Armed Forces Information Service, *The Armed Forces Officer* (Washington, D. C.: Department of Defense, 1988) p. 61 without paragraph indentation.

9. J. Robert Moskin, *The U.S. Marine Corps Story* (New York: McGraw-Hill Book Company, 1977) pp. 731–732 without paragraph indentation.

10. T. R. Fehrenbach, *This Kind of War* (New York: Bantam Books, 1991) p. 336 without paragraph indentation.

11. Millett, pp. 491–492.

12 *The Navy Cross: Vietnam*, edited by Paul D. Stevens (Forest Ranch, CA: Sharp and Dunnigan Publications, Inc., 1989) p. 272.

13. *The Congressional Medal of Honor: The Names, The Deeds* (Forest Ranch, CA: Sharp and Dunnigan Publications, Inc., 1984) p. 282 with additional paragraph indentation.

14. Armed Forces Information Service, *The Armed Forces Officer*, pp. 62–63.

15. Lieutenant General Victor H. Krulak, USMC (Ret.), *First to Fight: An Inside View of the U. S. Marine Corps* (Annapolis, MD: Naval Institute Press, 1984) p. 111.

16. Charles J. Quilter, *U.S. Marines in the Persian Gulf, 1990-1991: With the I Marine Expeditionary Force in Desert Shield and Desert Storm* (Washington, D.C.: History and Museums Division, Headquarters, U. S. Marine Corps) pp. 28–29.

17. *Ibid*, pp. 55–56.

18. Krulak, *First to Fight*, p. 67.

19. Millett, p. 333.

20. Moskin, p. 465.

21. *Ibid*, pp. 465–466.

22. *Ibid*, p. 464.

23. A reprint of the 1940 edition of this manual is available to Marine units as FMFRP 12-15 (PCN 100 013580 00).

24. Lieutenant General Victor A. Krulak, USMC (Ret.), "A Soldier's Dilemma," *Marine Corps Gazette* (November 1986) p. 24.

25. *Ibid*, pp. 29–31.

26. J. F. C. Fuller, *Generalship: Its Diseases and Their Cure* (Harrisburg, PA: Military Service Publishing Company, 1936) p. 86.

27. Jon T. Hoffman, *Once A Legend*: *"Red Mike" Edson of the Marine Raiders* (Novato, CA: Presidio Press, 1994) p. 249.

28. Krulak, *First to Fight*, p. 190.

29. Millett, p. 571.

30. Colonel Robert D. Heinl, Jr., USMC (Ret.), *The Marine Officer's Guide*, 4th ed. (Annapolis, MD: Naval Institute Press, 1977) p. 371.

31. *Ibid*, p. 374.

32. James B. Stockdale, Foreword to *Foundations of Moral Obligation* by Joseph G. Brennan (Newport, RI: Naval War College Press, 1992) p. xi.

33. *The Congressional Medal of Honor*, pp. 35-36. Paragraph indentations added.

34. Fehrenbach, p. 349.

35. Martin van Creveld, *Fighting Power: German and U.S. Army Performance, 1939-1945* (Westport, CN: Greenwood Press, 1982) p. 3. Van Creveld is the leading theorist of the concept of "fighting power," and the description contained herein builds on this earlier work.

## Epilogue

1. S. L. A. Marshall, *Man Against Fire* (Gloucester, MA: Peter Smith, 1978) p. 208.

2 Andrew Geer, *The New Breed* (Nashville, TN: The Battery Press, 1989) pp. 281–282 without paragraph indentations.

3. T. R. Fehrenbach, *This Kind of War* (New York: Bantam Books, 1991) p. 183.

4. This material was taken from a letter dated 8 October 1994 from William L. Henson to the Commandant of the Marine Corps.

5. Adapted from General Carl E. Mundy, Jr., "What Is It That Makes Marines?," *Marine Corps Gazette* (March 1993) p. 15 with minor textual changes.

6. Lieutenant General Victor H. Krulak, USMC (Ret.), *First To Fight: An Inside View of the U.S. Marine Corps* (Annapolis, MD: Naval Institute Press, 1984) p. 222.

## Marine Corps Manual

1. *Marine Corps Manual* (with changes 1 and 2 and message 122003Z Aug 87, ALMAR 178/87) (Washington D.C.: Department of the Navy, Headquarters U. S. Marine Corps, 1980) para. 1100, pp. 1–21.

## The Oaths

1. Admiral Arleigh Burke, USN, as quoted in Colonel Robert D. Heinl, Jr., USMC (Ret.), *The Marine Officer's Guide*, 4th ed. (Annapolis, MD: Naval Institute Press, 1977) p. 260.

2. James C. Gaston and Janis Bren Hietala, eds., *Ethics and National Defense: The Timeless Issues*, "The Officer's Oath: Words that Bind," by James H. McGrath (Washington, D. C.: National Defense University Press, 1993) pp. 27–28.

## Trust

1. *Marine Corps Manual,* para 1100.2d(1) adapted to include all Marine leaders.

49509285R00081

Made in the USA
Columbia, SC
22 January 2019